CONVERSATIONS WITH KESHAV

PART ONE

Vinay Sutaria

A catalogue record for this book is available from the British Library.

First Edition: September 2022

Paperback ISBN: 978-1-8381985-4-1
Hardcover ISBN: 978-1-8381985-3-4

For Pramukh Swami Maharaj
who gave me everything, and asked for nothing.
You are the most divine being to have ever existed.
I love you. I miss you.

CONTENTS

INTRODUCTION 6

SHANTI 17

SHARIR 31

SUKH 45

SWABHAV 65

SEVA 87

SADVICHAR 93

SAMJAN 107

SANKHYA 129

SAMP 141

SATSANG 157

SADHANA 167

SATPURUSH 179

SHASTRA 201

SHARNAGATI 215

SAR 221

INTRODUCTION

Struggle. Pain. Misery. These universal flaws of existence seem to affect every being on this planet. For some, the trials of life are overpowering. For others, a bored status quo prevails, and for a minority, mountains are pounded to dust in the search for meaning and happiness. Within the depths of every individual's heart, there is a deep yearning. A need to know *why*? Why are we alive? Why do we experience problems? Why are we here? In the search for answers to these uncertainties, who do we turn to? Where do we seek true clarity and inner solace?

For over five decades, HH Pramukh Swami Maharaj had perceived the pulse of individuals and society at large. He identified their areas of concern and presented them with practical solutions. This was possible due to his long-standing experience of having personally counselled thousands of people of all ages, from all strata of society.

Over the course of his lifetime, he delivered over 22,000 discourses to audiences ranging from two to over 200,000. He personally read and replied to over 750,000 letters, dealing with an incredibly wide range of personal, familial, business, social, and spiritual issues. In his mere presence, many experienced malice melting, doubts dissolving, confusions clearing, scars healing, prejudices perishing, and fears fleeing. He was not ranked as an outstanding orator, yet his sweet, soft voice, simple thoughts and spiritual experiences conveyed profound spiritual wisdom. Sometimes serious, sometimes humorous, his talks were listened to by thousands with pin drop silence. He led an austere life, absent of any personal gains or comfort. Possessing nothing, asking for nothing, wanting nothing, he went around giving his all. Despite his growing age and ailments, he tirelessly travelled from tiny tribal huts to modern metropolitan cities across the world, to promote lives full of virtues, shining with an uncommon brilliance of moral and spiritual power. His striking humility, profound wisdom and simplicity touched countless. His inherent love for humankind and respect towards all faiths weaved the fabric of cultural unity, interfaith harmony, and universal peace. But the sole reason behind his unique success was his deep, unbroken association with God.

As one who had spent their entire life in the service of others, Pramukh Swami's teachings were accepted by all as being above any self-interest or bias. His words resonated with profound philosophical insight that provided practical guidance. But the main reason why his words were received with so much trust was that he *lived* every word that he preached.

As one who spends their entire life in the service of others, Mahant Swami Maharaj's teachings are accepted by all. They are above any self-interest or bias. His words resonate with profound philosophical insight. He lives every single word that he preaches. Every word of his is already an integral part of his life. Mahant Swami reaches out to one and all through spiritual travels, festivals, public assemblies, personal meetings, correspondence and phone calls. During these encounters countless have experienced inner joy, peace and tranquility; solutions are found to life's most crucial questions; unique virtues are inspired; and divine faith is developed in one and all. Mahant Swami's discourses and teachings are born out of deep reflection, unique insight and divine experience. He is soft-spoken and his discourses, based on the teachings of Bhagwan Swaminarayan and his spiritual successors, particularly those of Yogiji Maharaj and Pramukh Swami Maharaj, guide and inspire a wide range of audiences across the globe.

But why *Conversations with Keshav*? Like a turtle that retracts its limbs into its body, some have observed how Keshav withdraws from a flurry of activities and in an instant, comes to rest within himself. Some find him as light as a feather, even under mountains of work; and as fresh as the morning dew, even after rigorous exertion. Many have witnessed him totally free and natural amidst a hustling crowd of thousands, and just as leisured and casual in moments of solitude. In the most stormy times, some have found him absolutely calm, composed and collected. Some have observed a fragile tenderness in him, others a tough troubleshooter; some a powerful yet yielding nature. Some have found him totally untouched by the world – like a lotus amidst the water. Some find him whole and complete – leaving nothing on site or undone. Some admire his total surrender to God, his elevated state, his equilibrium, loyalty, contentment, and his cheerfulness through unrest and illness. He is an icon of purity. An image of enthusiasm. A monument of compassion. The manifestation of beauty. The embodiment of truth. He is the perfect personification of perfect divinity.

The ancient Hindu scriptures reflect the reality of existence through the story of Parikshit. A noble and humble king, Parikshit was overcome by the influences of vices and pleasures. Under this influence, once upon visiting a sage's hut in the forest, he was furious when the sage didn't get up to greet him. Angered, he tossed a dead snake over the neck of the sage. Cutting a long story short, the sage's son cursed Parikshit to die within seven days for committing such a heinous crime. When Parikshit was informed of this curse, he became aware of his mortality and transformed his life for the better within seven days.

Today, we are all Parikshit today. Parikshit lives on in each one of us. How? All of us are going to die within seven days – there is no eighth day in the week. When Parikshit became aware of his death, he conversed with Shukdevji, listening to his talks attentively. In the same way, we will converse with Keshav and become aware of reality – as it is.

Wherever you choose to look – history, psychology, social sciences or anthropology – all of them point us towards five common human strivings. The first being the search for happiness. Not just happiness, but we search for *permanent* happiness, and that too, without any misery. Reality check: we never get it. Twenty years ago, not many had heard of air conditioning, and today every car has it. Not only that, but with a press of a remote, or a touch on your mobile's screen, the climate is set to your liking. But how long do you really remain 'happy'? Whilst we're on the topic of cars, think about garages. Before, we had to get out the car and open them; today they have become automatic. We even have speed limiters in our vehicles, to ensure we don't go crazy! How much we have done for our comfort – for our happiness – yet we've come full circle. This is just one aspect of human life.

Another human striving is fame. Humans want to make a lasting mark amidst their finite existence. We seek to make our place in the world. Whether that is through our career, philanthropy, family, or a personal legacy – we want to make our name. The third is infinite knowledge. As advanced creatures of existence, humans are not satisfied by pleasures and comfort alone, we want to *know* things. We believe that the more we know, the more we grow. We do... but only to a certain extent. Fourth is freedom. Interestingly, despite being moderately 'free' compared to all other creatures on this planet, humans still feel 'trapped' and do whatever is within their ability to seek freedom. This isn't seen just on an individual level, but on a global level too. Every country wants to be 'free' and 'independent'. It is an intrinsic need of the human mind.

Finally, we have status. Humans seek power. We may not get it at work, so we attempt to seek it at home. If we don't get it there, we seek it within our friend circles, and continue to progress until one day we ourselves physically become powerless. If we truly contemplate on it, all of humanity strives to seek these five goals, just in different ways. And it is this search itself that, paradoxically, leads us to misery...

To accommodate for a wider audience, I have tried to be reader-friendly in rendering Sanskrit and other non-English words into English. Traditionally, diacritical marks are used to distinguish between long and short vowels. I have tried to avoid this for the most part. Throughout the text, the diacritic 'ā' is used to indicate the long 'a' (as in c*a*r). For uniformity, some non-English words have been standardised and simplified throughout the text. Most definitions of non-English words have been given within the text itself. For non-English names of people and places, I have used the common Anglicised spelling.

This book is my humble attempt in seeking answers. Answers to the most fundamental questions that consume each and every individual on this planet. Just as a note to you, as the reader, this book does not demand to be read from cover to cover. The topics within stand alone, but, of course, concepts and ideas may be better understood when read in order. I leave this choice up to you.

I have tried my best to make this book, and the ideas within, as simple and straightforward as possible. The thoughts and ideas presented are clear, because Keshav himself is clear. To understand his words, you have to understand his silence too. This book is not a self-help book that is sugar-coated with wisdom and exercises. Thoughts and ideas within are often left open-ended, leaving you to deal with some ambiguity and interpretation. If you require any clarification in regards to any of the text, do reach out to me via email at **hello@vinaysutaria.com**.

Whilst reading this book, keep an open mind. I hope that through these conversations, certain thoughts, feelings, reason, and emotions that I feel are also evoked within you. Take your time understanding and contemplating on the conversations. Enjoy the process. Feel free to highlight, underline, and make notes throughout. This, to me, is a sign of an engaged reader. Make as many notes as possible – in the margins, in your notebooks, post-it notes, wherever. If any thoughts and ideas from this book stand out and resonate with you, please feel free to share them with others. Post pictures, stories and videos of your favourite conversations, quotes, sections and experiences on social media. Use the **#VinaySutaria** or **#TheKeshavWay**, so I can see them too!

Over the course of many years, HH Mahant Swami Maharaj has discoursed plenty on the topics related to mind, body and soul. Not only him, but the entire lineage of spiritual successors of Bhagwan Shri Swaminarayan, have all touched upon the deepest questions that dwell within our minds and hearts. This book is a culmination of that wisdom. And so, whatever advice you take away from these conversations is solely that of my gurus. If any other ideas or concepts here go uncredited, it was never my intention to do so, but rather, these ideas have become integral in my thinking and ideology. Whatever is good herein is that of my teachers; whatever is bad, is mine.

I apologise in advance for every instance in this book where you may feel offended. This was never my intention. These are my own views and interpretations, and they are mine alone. I also apologise for the male-dominated 'subject' of some of the text – this is merely indicative of the period in which parts were written or spoken, and are not a reflection of anyone's beliefs, intended target market, or any other underlying motive. I do not declare that I am free of biases and afflictions, and I am certainly not immune to making mistakes in my writing. If any errors of fact are noted, I would be grateful to be notified, so that future editions of this book can be corrected and updated.

Peace, happiness and true freedom are not things to be sought in some distant land or reserved for the afterlife, for they exist within each one of us – at this very moment – in fact, they exist at every breath and step you take. I wrote this book because I needed it more than anyone else. I wrote this book because I had many questions. I wrote this book because my questions were answered. The pages that follow reflect this.

Before we start, I would like to offer my due apologies. Not in being modest or polite, but in being obliged to accept the inadequacy and limitation of myself in portraying the magnanimity and intensity of Pramukh Swami and Mahant Swami. That is, in portraying who Keshav is. And so, whilst remembering my beloved gurus, I offer my deepest gratitude and prayers for you and your loved ones. May we all discover and connect to Keshav.

Vinay Sutaria
September 2022
Kedarnath, India

With many questions on my mind, I sat on the cool marble floor surrounding the exterior of the Yogi Smruti Mandir in Gondal. A fairly small but historical princely city, Gondal was once ruled by a powerful Rajput dynasty. It lies around 45km south of Rajkot, Gujarat. It was in this city that Gunatitanand Swami – the first spiritual successor of Bhagwan Shri Swaminarayan – left his mortal body. It was in this city that the guru of my guru, Yogiji Maharaj's final rites were performed. That is when it hit me again. The entire event, once again, became vivid in my mind.

Tens of thousands of people watched Mahant Swami hold the burning straw in both hands as he slowly circumambulated the funeral pyre. Senior swāmis (ordained monks) followed suit. According to traditional Hindu custom, Mahant Swami set alight the logs of sweet smelling wood, entrusting to the flames the mortal body of his spiritual master, who he had himself served for a number of decades. As the flames rose and crackled, the heat pushed him back several steps. He then slowly continued to circumambulate the pyre. There was complete silence. And amidst the crackling of the fire, cries could be heard from all corners of the campus. Mahant Swami and senior swamis watched lost in thought. Their half-grown beards masked their silent grief.

For those who had served Pramukh Swami from a distance, the transition may not have been problematic as such. Who am I to say? But for those who had physically served and spent time with him from close quarters, mind-wrenching questions must have arose. It was but natural. I was one of them. United to Pramukh Swami by body, mind and soul, it was for him that we lived and breathed. But now he did not. Thoughts of his passing – the inevitable – had never been entertained. Why would they? Who else could there be for us but Pramukh Swami Maharaj?

Pramukh Swami Maharaj was no ordinary being. He knew that his passing would cause considerable anguish to countless across the world. For some time he had quietly, and not so quietly, hinted of his going and the identity of his successor. Senior swamis now mulled over these words and gradually began to accept that life had to continue and that, in matter of fact, Pramukh Swami had not left them. After all, they had already experienced such a situation, forty-five years before, right here in Gondal.

It was the ultimate test of their understanding. If they had seen the divine in Pramukh Swami, they would recognise that same divinity present in Mahant Swami. Confusion and grief were but natural at the loss of the one to whom you had dedicated your life. But the awareness that the loved one had not really departed – that he was fully manifest within another – and that *he* would continue to guide, love and comfort was true spiritual understanding. This signified mature devotion.

Mahant Swami himself was not insensitive to these emotions. From the spiritual sense, of course, he was above all emotions and moods. But today, in fact, he was unassuming and straightforward. On his part there were never any declarations of authority or claims to successorship. Thousands began to experience Pramukh Swami within him and spontaneously accepted him as guru. No election. No vote. No canvassing. No such tradition exists in this fellowship. The succeeding guru has always been pointed to by the previous guru. No groups formed to disturb the harmony and unity. There was one family, and it unswervingly followed Mahant Swami Maharaj. It makes me remember the words uttered by Mahant Swami after the passing of Yogiji Maharaj when he reminisced: "When Yogi Bapa went to Akshardham I thought, 'That's it… the play is finished! The game is over!' But Pramukh Swami gradually took up the work in such a way that before I knew it, I was coupled to him."

It says much for Pramukh Swami's spiritual prowess, his ability to infuse honest spiritual values and ambitions, that no swami or devotee made claims to be Pramukh Swami's successor. There were no fights for property or temples. No quarrel for the 'throne' or for worship. Throughout history, the world has witnessed the decline of dynasties and of untold competent institutions founded by sincere spiritual masters. The reasons being plenty – from petty bickering, ego, or even the desire for luxurious living – but not here. There is *something* here. Something truly amazing that keeps me knocking at his door. And here I was again. Mahant Swami was right here in Gondal. I wanted answers to all of my questions. I had got them. I put my pen to the paper and began to write as I recalled every conversation with Keshav…

शान्ति:

Shanti

[shaan-tee]

inner peace or fulfilment

Difficulties. Unease. Misery. They don't just affect the superpowers and nations of this planet. Hostilities exist on a more dangerous and worrying level. A deadly unrest brews in every home and heart. Herbert Hoover, the 31st President of the USA famously said: "Peace is not made at the council table or by treaties, but in the hearts of men." John F. Kennedy proclaimed: "The mere absence of war is not peace. Peace is a daily, a weekly, a monthly process, gradually changing opinions, slowly eroding old barriers, quietly building new structures." The UN constitution reads: "Since wars begin in the minds of men, it is in the minds of men that defences of peace must be constructed." How do we find peace in our lives? Where do we go? To whom do we go?

KESHAV: Pramukh Swami Maharaj used to say that it is hard-work plus prayers that equal success. Everyone seeks success but it seems so distant. Many progress on the exterior, but not within. Look at Napoleon! He said that he had not seen six happy days in his life!

External success is only partial. Success at its best is when one's life and character is at its best. True success is balance in life. Chanakya said that whatever a man intends on doing, it should be done by him with wholehearted and strenuous effort. This is how work should be done – with wholeheartedness. Churchill, Tolstoy and many others… they did a lot [externally], they put in the hard work, but they didn't get the ultimate striving they desired – peace.

ME: Isn't peace and success what we all seek?

KESHAV: (nodding) The entire world. Every human. Everyone is drowned in the ocean of misery and unease. Michael Jackson had so much! What did he say? He said that there is probably no one as unhappy as him in the whole world! You see, comfort and happiness are two different things. Always remember that. Temporary happiness can only give temporary peace, but it can never give lasting inner peace.

There is a Hindi saying: 'do din ki chāndni, phir andheri rāt' (our happiness is temporary). Material contentment can only bring some level of peace in our life. Permanent peace can *only* be derived from prāpti no vichār (the contemplation of attainment). The soul seeks peace. But, instead of giving it the fuel it needs, we choose to feed it with the temporary pleasures available to us in this world. True peace lies only in God and Guru.

ME: What should I do to experience peace in life?

KESHAV: Pramukh Swami Maharaj said: "We shall experience peace and happiness, mutual love and good feelings when we realise that God resides in each and every one of us." He also said: "By making others unhappy one cannot gain peace. By making others happy, and helping others benefit, we only gain and become happy. In the good of others, lies our own. In the happiness of others lies our own. This is an eternal law."

True success is to experience peace within. Having a [spiritual] understanding bestows one with peace. It is when one has such an understanding that all types of personal pain and misery dissolve. One also needs to understand God to be genuine and satsang to be bona fide.

ME: Sometimes those around us do not let us experience peace. Then…?

KESHAV: Vidur said to Yudhisthir: "Those who control their senses acquire the sovereignty of the entire world." The solution to all the problems you face are to be resolved within *your* own mind. If you want inner peace, then even if the fault is 90 percent of another person, and only ten percent yours, you must focus on that ten percent. *That* is within your control. It is only *that* which you can change. Agreements always brings results and arguments always leads to more arguments. In agreement, one experiences enduring peace.

One who sees one's own faults [and makes a conscious effort to remove them] will ultimately attain peace. But one who sees the faults of others is a sinner in the eyes of God, and they will only experience unease. By seeing the virtues of others, one experiences peace. By looking at the faults of others, one experiences inner turmoil. Yogi Bapa said: "The key to peace is to see everything and everyone as divine." That is it. See divinity everywhere. Let me ask you something. Do you believe that peace is in detachment?

ME: I believe it. But whether I act based on it and live by that truth... I don't know.

KESHAV: I am saying this, but whether you experience it or not is a different matter. Tell me, do you find peace in eating or in not eating?

ME: Eating? There is no much happiness like there is in food!

KESHAV: (laughing gently) Ninety percent of people believe that there is happiness in indulgence. The ancient sages tell us that it is through detaching from such indulgences that we can experience happiness and peace. If you really act upon this, your miseries and troubles will be cleansed right here. In detachment and learning to let go, there is immense peace.

ME: But we live in this world. We are immersed in it. How do we 'detach'?

KESHAV: Yes, you are immersed in the world. This may go against your normal experiences. But look throughout history and you will see that man has ran after wealth, status, women [or men], and power. Every human. Have they experienced peace?

ME: Deep down we know this, we hear it, but we don't experience peace... why? How can there be happiness and peace in not indulging and detaching?

KESHAV: I was once delivering a talk in a town in the USA and when I finished, a man came up to me and told me that the ancient sages were fools. I asked him why he thought this way. Did he interview them? Did he ever meet them? So, how could he spontaneously make such a judgement?

The ancient sages may not have made airplanes or cars, or even any form of technology, but nor did they need them. They were content with what they had. We are not at peace in the modern world and so we create and indulge. Despite everything humanity has achieved, we still feel dissatisfied. Always. Necessity is the mother of invention. All inventions have been created because of 'need'. Despite 'needs' being fulfilled, why does the solution seem so distant even today? Statistics show that every ten years, crime doubles. Two thousand people commit suicide every single day. Rape, murder, theft... all figures seem to keep going up. Is this true progress? The only thing progressing is the figures!

ME: But why is that? Why is humanity not progressing in the true sense?

KESHAV: Our endeavours are in the wrong direction. The search for peace itself is not wrong, but the direction we are heading is wrong. This is all because of our mind. We don't believe the ancient sages or the Guru as we should. We only have superficial understanding. To cross the ocean of this world, we *need* the Satpurush.[1] Napoleon

---

[1] the bonafide Guru; also referred to as Sādhu, Sant, or, Motāpurush

said: "I have everything under the sun at my feet, yet I have not seen six happy days in my life." This is not just hearsay, it is written! Think about *who* is saying this. Napoleon! He had a huge empire! People really believed that he was great and happy, yet he said this, from his own experience. Aurangzeb too. He had one of the greatest Mughal empires, yet on his deathbed he lamented that his whole life had gone to waste. He put his own father in prison and killed his brother for the throne. Even then, at the end of his life he regretted everything and called himself a sinner – 'meri sāri zindagāni fazool gai' (my whole life has gone to waste).

This pattern is seen throughout history. Man lives, but he does not live. Whatever one does is to fuel the ego and to show off to others – to make an impression on others. And, for most, this is how life just passes.

ME: The people who have done this, why haven't they thought once to look for the true source of inner peace and happiness?

KESHAV: It's not just them. Even today, the vast majority fail to realise that there is no lasting happiness in this world. We fluctuate between happiness and misery continuously. For the past five minutes I have been saying that there is peace in detachment, and you nodded your head a few times, but when you are alone, why do you walk in the opposite direction? This is a lack of faith. Clear this fact today. You may have faith, but you do not have *firm* faith.

ME: (unable to meet eyes with him) You're right... I lack firm faith. Even though I know I should have faith, it often feels like I'm on the fence...

KESHAV: First understand this. Have firm faith in the words of God and Guru. We readily believe a doctor when they tell us to stop eating something, or if they tell us to follow certain guidance, but why is it that here we think, 'āp bak bak, hum soon soon' (you keep talking, we will just listen)? Experiences of inner peace don't just happen like that. You need zeal, faith and perseverance in life too. It takes time.

The Guru's life speaks for itself! His life is one of profound experience. His life proves to us that there is peace in detachment. We only feel good when we shower in hot water; when we eat the most immaculate dishes and indulge in various cuisines; when we have the best car or the biggest home... with such expectations how can we expect to experience peace and happiness? Look towards at the Guru! Despite being surrounded with all possible pleasures of this world, all within arm's reach, the Guru remains detached. He experiences true peace continuously.

You've heard the story of Buddha, right? He had all the pleasures in the world. He didn't experience any misery himself as such, but he witnessed the misery of others and renounced his future kingdom. Maharaj[2] says in [Vachanamrut][3] Vartal 16: "If there is

---

[2] throughout, 'Maharaj' refers to Bhagwan Shri Swaminarayan
[3] the compilation of the spiritual discourses of Bhagwan Shri Swaminarayan

bliss in ruling a kingdom, then why would great kings such as Swāyambhuv Manu[4] and others leave their kingdoms and go into the forests to perform austerities? If there is bliss in women [or men for women], then why would King Chiktraketu[5] abandon ten million women?" Isn't *this* worth pondering on itself?

ME: Yes... So faith is everything?

KESHAV: Yes. [Vachanamrut] Sarangpur 9: "If one has intense faith, one can be liberated here on earth itself." Put all your own experiences to one side and hold on to the experiences of the Satpurush, because they are always in line with the scriptures. Shastriji Maharaj said: 'vyāp tetlo santāp' (the more you possess, the more you will suffer [miseries]). Anyone who has given too much predominance to themselves [believing themselves to be the body] has eventually suffered. Those who have strived for the soul have met with peace. There is no happiness in the indulgence of pleasures.

ME: But we do experience *some* pleasure and joy...

KESHAV: That belief is itself moha (delusion). Why don't we learn from history? History might not repeat itself, but it does rhyme. Elvis Presley had so much, yet it is believed he committed suicide in the end. What about Marilyn Monroe? The same. This entire life is

---

[4] the mind born son of Brahmā; the first Manu
[5] a pious king mentioned in the Shrimad Bhagavata Purana

full of misery. Some study for twenty odd years of our life to barely make an income to sustain themselves and they call that true happiness? There may be *some* happiness, but there is always more unhappiness – that is what Gunatitanand Swami said. Cravings never cease, so fulfilment from pleasures are never met. It is a never-ending cycle. Only the Satpurush is the living example of peace.

A reporter from London once asked Yogi Bapa[6] if he had ever become sad, upset or depressed about anything in life. Yogiji Maharaj instantly replied: "Never once in my life!" I was right there with him! When we look at the life of Yogi Bapa it wouldn't seem that there was much joy or peace in his life, but he was above all of this. When we learn to detach, only then do we experience the true bliss of God inherent to all of us.

Everyone wants to experience peace within, and there are two ways to experience it. One is to worship God, second is to believe God to be the all-doer. Maharaj has said: "Whether you experience joy or misery, remain stable minded, as I will look after those with such understanding like they are my own."

Keep your focus on God, and ups and downs will just pass by. Learn to tolerate in life. Remain patient and courageous and you will move forward and overcome difficulties. Pray to God and remain patient in life. With tolerance, you can overcome any difficulty with utmost faith in God.

---

[6] the fourth spiritual successor of Bhagwan Swaminarayan; the guru of Mahant Swami Maharaj

ME: Faith in God and his all-doership? Like whatever happens, happens for the best?

KESHAV: Whatever happens is *always* for the best. Devanand Swami writes: "Dhiraj dhar tu are adhirā." Maintain forbearance and patience, regardless of whatever challenges you face in life. If we keep patience, everything will be accomplished. Pass over all our worries to our God. Whatever God does is always for the best. God provides everyone as per their needs — an ant and elephant both receive food as required. However much is required, God provides accordingly, but nevertheless, he provides for everyone.

The only thing you need to do is keep patience. If you keep patience then you can attain everything. You attain peace. You attain happiness. You attain everything that needs to be required. The Pandavas[7] faced difficulties and misery, but what did they do? They maintained patience. That is why God became pleased with them and showered them with bliss and peace.

ME: Should I pray to God asking for peace, or is that wrong? Is that selfish?

KESHAV: (shaking his head) Of course not. *Absolutely* you should pray. That is the only medium through which you can help ease the burden of the troubles that you face.

---

[7] the five sons of Pandu in the Mahabharat

ME: Where can I find peace of mind – in money and pleasures or in God?

KESHAV: Money is rooted in greed. Greed causes strife. Only spirituality gives one peace. God is the source of all peace and harmony. People feel they experience peace upon receiving perishable objects, but it is only followed by pain when they lose them. Attachment is the source of misery. On the other hand, when one receives the wealth of God [in the form of understanding], one receives true happiness.

ME: What is the way to attain everlasting peace of mind?

KESHAV: Through daily prayer and reading the shastras (scriptures). By doing a little every day, our mind will become calm. Like I said, realise God as the all-doer. Whatever happens in life is only for your own benefit. 'I was probably heading towards trouble and God saved me' – by maintaining such a thought process, you will never be shocked or upset in times of failure or disappointment.

Our efforts never go in vain. Sometimes, if we don't succeed, we should think that it is for the best. That way we will not become frustrated. By offering daily prayer and satsang[8] our mind experiences peace.

_____

[8] the practice of spiritual association with the ātmā, God, Satpurush and the sacred scriptures

ME: When we face difficulties, we feel unease, the opposite of peace! It seems that the more we acquire and get, the more unease we feel. Then it only feels natural to complain to those around us, or for me, to complain to you...

KESHAV: Does complaining ever resolve miseries? Does it make it disappear? Instead, learn to leave your worries to God. Always live within your means. Never exceed your means. Live simply. Wear simple clothes. The truth feels bitter. Only do what is feasible within your means. Do not spend extravagantly. Do not spend your time or money on futile things.

Materialism has increased and we end up with less savings. This leads to misery. However, there is no misery if you imbibe samjan (spiritual knowledge). What I am saying is that you should always stay within the āgnā (spiritual commands) of God. If we take refuge in God, he shows us compassion. This is the true principle.

God always protects us. Perhaps, further difficulties would have arisen if our wishes were fulfilled. We may have had to suffer further hardships, so they did not happen. We should place all our desires and wishes at the feet of God. He will remove all our deficiencies. Keep patience, maintain refuge in God, and practice satsang. There is no other solution for peace but to maintain unwavering faith in God. This, along with knowledge, is the key to peace.

शरीर

Sharir

[shuh-ree-ra]

the material body or bodies

The great fifth century Indian poet, Kalidas, writes: 'shariramādyam khalu dharmasādhanam' (this body is surely the *foremost* instrument of performing [good] deeds).[1] In any area of human endeavour, our body plays the most important role. It is through our body that we interact with the world around us. We all have a body, but it is important for us to have a *healthy* body. Mahant Swami, for decades, has promoted healthy living, not for the sake of becoming body conscious, but to enable us to become spiritually conscious, through this rare human birth...

BODY

KESHAV: Health is wealth. The body progresses as long as we keep it in shape. If the body is kept healthy, the mind remains healthy. If the mind becomes healthy and pure, we are in a position to elevate ourselves spiritually, and thus, we can experience peace and joy in life. Our scriptures say that there is nothing more valuable than the human birth, yet life passes by so quickly and many waste away their life.

ME: But if I focus on the body, doesn't that make me body conscious?

KESHAV: Gunatitanand Swami has said that the body is the home of illness. Diseases are latent in the body. People may look well, but within, there are diseases which may

---

[1] kumārasambhava 5.33

become troublesome at any time. This is the way of the world – some days bring joy, while other days bring misery. But in order to elevate ourselves spiritually, engage in bhakti (devotion) and sevā (selfless service), the body must be kept healthy.

ME: That makes sense. Are there any particular causes for ill health?

KESHAV: There are four reasons for bad health. The first is swabhāvik (inherited or genetic). We see individuals with heart disease, diabetes, and other such disorders. They maintain a healthy body and routine, yet they have bad health! This is swabhāvik, and normally we can't do much for these types of diseases other than to follow the guidance of medical professionals and maintain diet control.

The second is akasmātik (accidental). I think this speaks for itself. We can meet with accidents or risks and dangers. Then something happens and we develop bad health. Third, we have kāyik (one's own bodily actions). If people do not take care of themselves, and put themselves at risk, then it is all but natural for them to develop bad health. And finally, we have the most important reason which is often not clearly understood – mānsik (stemming from the mind). Due to our swabhāvs (base natures) such as anger, lust, greed, we can develop bad health. More and more research talks about stress and the effects it has on health. This is mānsik. According to Ayurveda, it is rooted in pitta (bodily heat) and is predominant in the youth today, which we see when many develop regular headaches, acidity, ulcers and the likes.

ME: How does one maintain good health – both physical and mental?

KESHAV: Listen clearly. This guidance is priceless. No one told me this in my childhood, if only they did! Firstly, I cannot stress how useful prānāyama is for your health. Along with this, you should have āhār-vivek (dietary discretion). This is key for good health. What to eat, how much to eat, when to eat, and even where to eat. I mean this both literally and also by what we take in through our senses. By taking in pure 'food' [through the senses], inner unrest and misery that has accumulated over countless births is destroyed. The antahkarana (the Vedic mind) is purified and good thoughts arise in the mind. You probably don't want to hear all this... (laughing softly)

ME: No, I honestly want to hear more! Please carry on?

KESHAV: You need awareness. In a hundred percent stomach, you should allow 50 percent for food, 25 percent for water, and leave 25 percent empty [to allow for digestion]. Maharaj himself said to his sādhus: "Don't eat according to the hunger of the mind, but according to the hunger of the stomach." This is what he meant. Hippocrates, one of the pioneering thinkers of Western medicine, said: "Let thy food be thy medicine." Nishkulanand also said: "There is no medicine like that of discipline in eating." Yogi Bapa went one step further and said that fasting is medicine! He used to say that no one dies from fasting, but people die from eating! There is so much to say about health!

ME: Another time?

KESHAV: (nodding with a beautiful smile) Yes, another time...

ME: Who am I?

KESHAV: First you need self-knowledge. You are not just this body. We are made up of three things: the body, the mind and the soul. If the soul leaves the body, everything ends. The mind forms part of the body. Both are perishable. Kabir has said: "What is great about this body or any wealth when, in the end, it all turns to dust?"

One [body] you think you are (the mind), the second [body] people think you are (the physical body), and the third [body] is who you really are (the soul). The soul – the ātmā – has no caste, creed, nationality or difference. *That* is who you really are. It is the identification with the body that is the root cause of the misery of humankind. Maharaj himself has said: "The root of all sins is the body."

You may be whatever else, but you are not the body! The mind commands, the body obeys. The mind says get up, the body gets up! The mind says eat, the body eats! What is happening here? It is always the mind ordering. The Shrimad Bhagavata Purana proclaims: "The false belief of being the body hinders the attainment of such a state and one is actually oblivious of one's own ātmā."[2] It is also the cause of our fault-finding nature! Maharaj says: "Those who believe the body and ātmā to be one see faults in others." When we say *my* house' are we the house itself, or are we the owner of the house? When we say *my* body' are we the body, or are we the owner of the body?

It's simple, yet, if you ask anyone in this world who they are, they point to themselves – to this chunk of flesh and bones – to their own body! But they're not! We fail to realise that we are the owner of the body that we have. Look around at the world right now, everyone behaves as if they are the body. The whole world! We don't behave as the soul, only the Guru behaves as the soul. Do you get it?

ME: I think I kind of understand…?

KESHAV: We say *my* mind, *my* body, *my* house. When we say 'my', two relations arise – the possessed and the possessor. When we say 'my house', who is the possessor and what is possessed? When we say 'my body', who is the possessor and what is possessed? No one seems to think about this. People are born, they grow, and they die – all without the knowledge of who they truly are! People pass away just like any other animal on this planet. If you don't have knowledge of your own soul, you are no better than an animal. In fact, your whole life is wasted!

---

[2] Shrimad Bhagavata Purana 3.7.11–12

On 5th July 1991, at a psychiatrists conference in Bristol, Prince Charles addressed a seminar of FRCP doctors saying: "I believe the *most urgent need* for Western man is to rediscover that divine element in his being, without which there can never be any possible hope or meaning to our existence in this earthly realm." This is what Pramukh Swami has been exemplifying and teaching us for years! The ancient sages went in, in, in, and science kept going out, out, out! Both are scientists in the truest sense. That divine being is your soul. Without the knowledge of the soul, you can never be happy. Facts are facts. You cannot fool around with such things.

In a game of chess, it doesn't matter if you play as the king, queen, or the pawn, at the end of the game, all the pieces end up in the same box. The king and the pawn go back into the same box when the game is over. Napoleon, Akbar, Solomon – all have ended in dust. Once the soul leaves this body, nothing remains. What you see of this physical body today – nothing will remain. That is why such wisdom has to be engrained in the jiva[3], so that one experiences peace, happiness and joy in life. Otherwise, you will only encounter misery.

Dehabhimān (the illusion of identifying yourself to be one with the body) is the prime cause of all suffering and misery. Know that you are not the body. There are no labels

---

[3] 'that which is living', derived from the verb-root 'jiv' – to live. Often used synonymously with ātmā – the individual, embodied soul still bound by māyā

whatsoever to your true identity. You are infinitely powerful and limitless. Shukdevji[4] said to King Parikshit: "Get rid of your animal-like mentality that you are going to die. You may leave this body, but the ātmā lives on."

MIND

KESHAV: A lot has been written about the mind. The whole field of psychology is focused on the mind. The East have always focused on the mind and soul, it has been soul conscious. The West has seemed to fixate on the body, it has been body conscious. If the mind is unstable, life becomes unstable.

When we visited Nairobi with Yogi Bapa, we visited the home of a wealthy family. After entering their home, we saw a large cage and inside it there was a teenage boy growling and making noises. Yogi Bapa questioned: "Who is that and why is he in the cage?" The individual whose house it was told us that it was his son and he was in the cage because he was mentally unstable. He would harm anyone who touched him. Yogi Bapa asked: "Even you as the father?" The man replied: "Swami! My child doesn't even know that I'm his father!" Now look at this... you may have all the wealth in the world, but without a stable mind, it is all worthless and meaningless. All the problems in the world stem from a smoked [dirty] mind. Man has gone from fighting with stones to

---

[4] an ancient sage; the son of Veda Vyas

fighting with nuclear weapons, but man has failed to improve his mind. The greatest research of this century is that you can change your life by changing the attitude of your mind. We may change our cars, homes, clothes... this is all fine, but the most significant change that has to be made is within your own mind.

We talk about a healthy mind but do we really believe that a healthy mind is more important than a healthy body? Unless you do, nothing I say here will affect you. We seem to be able to monitor and nourish every part of our body, but why is it that we often fail to do the same for our minds?

There are over fifty professions in the medical field that deal with the body, and for the mind there is only psychology and psychiatry. We really don't seem to believe that a healthy mind is more important than a healthy body. When we do accept that both are equal, we will change within ourselves. The body is visible and physical, whereas the mind is invisible and subtle. Sometimes in life, the things that are invisible and more important than that which is visible.

We see buildings, but not their foundations. We see food and water, but not the air that they are made up of. We see planets, galaxies and stars, but we don't see the gravity which keeps everything in cosmic order. We see wonderful, beautiful creations, but we shouldn't have to worry about seeing the creator. Why? Because the things that are invisible are more important than that which is visible.

Even the world of science is founded on concepts which are invisible. Buildings stand erect, bridges stay stable, planes and rockets fly. Why? Because of engineers? They stand because of the calculations made by the engineers! Calculations are nothing more than numbers and symbols. Both are concepts of the mind. They are *all* concepts which are invisible, but because science accepts them, buildings stand erect, bridges remain stable, and planes and rockets fly. The world of the mind is found on concepts which are invisible. There are also the concepts of emotion: love, fear, sorrow, joy. We don't see them, but we feel them. They are found on the concepts of values, philosophy and truth.

Around 5000 years ago, the Indian sages clearly explained the nature of the mind. They even went to the extent of explaining the four functions of the mind. Manas for thinking and inspiration; buddhi is not just intellect, it also selects and discriminates between good and bad thoughts; chitta affirms thoughts, contemplates and visualises; and finally, ahamkara is what leads to identification with one's thoughts and actions, giving us a sense of identity. So, the mind is responsible for creating your identity. Identity is more important than attitude. The stability of your mind is the most important aspect of your life.

Allopathy says that 80 percent of disease stems from the mind. This is true. Chronic illnesses often begin within the mind because of things that we cling on to. There is a direct link between the mind and the immune system. They are *densely* related. If your immune system is strong, you are protected from disease. Protect your mind and you protect your immune system. If your mind is strong, nothing will affect you. Until recently, science has done a lot for the body, but unfortunately it has not done enough for the mind. This is changing now gradually. External factors influence our mind a lot. Your mind is everything. An impure mind leads to an impure life. A pure mind leads to a pure life. The key to a pure mind is satsang.

ME: I constantly experience mental anguish. I confide in you about this, but it's like I'm constantly battling with my mind. How can the mind be harnessed?

KESHAV: Shri Krishna says that it is the mind of an individual that is the cause of both bondage and liberation.[5] By engaging the mind in the nine forms of bhakti (devotion), the diseases of the mind can be cured. The nature of the mind is such that it will *always* desire worldly pleasures and try to deceive us, but if we engage it in bhakti and satsang, it gradually becomes purified and stable. That is why we say that we have to *fight* our mind. We should bombard it. Our weapon is āgnā (spiritual commands). The mind should never be free to retaliate. Then will it not be destroyed? Bhagatji Maharaj said: "Although the antahkarana[6] may seem to be tranquil from our point of view, when we encounter circumstances where we are praised or insulted, ripples – in the form of thoughts – will arise."

---

[5] Bhagavad Gita 6.5
[6] the mind, comprising of four different faculties, according to Hindu philosophy

It all hinges on controlling one's mind and disciplining one's senses. Only those who conquer their mind are considered brave. Diseases of the body will come and go, but mental anguish can never be cured easily. The mind always has loops. Mental misery will never come to an end, no matter how many material objects or pleasures you indulge in, you will *never* feel satisfied. The desire for worldly pleasures *must* be overcome. Maharaj himself says that those who desire bodily pleasures and preserve them will remain forever in misery, but they do not think about this. One can imprint any thoughts in the mind, and the jiva becomes inclined in that way. Without it, there is no peace. To win over the mind, one *needs* satsang.

SOUL

KESHAV: Rising above the body and the mind, we should remain one with God and engage in all activities. If we get something, it is God's wish, if we lose it, that too is God's wish. In such understanding, and in behaving as the ātmā, there is no burden. There is only bliss.

ME: I am the ātmā...

KESHAV: Understanding *that* is 80 percent of all sādhanā (spiritual endeavour). This itself is jnān (spiritual knowledge). Rumi said: "I lost everything and found myself." You are the soul. It's not simply about believing. It is about realising.

Maharaj said that one who believes their jivātmā (the soul in its state of ignorance) to be distinct from the three bodies – gross, subtle and causal – and who believes God forever resides within them, behaves as the ātmā. Spiritually, he is constantly alert and believes that God resides within. The jiva is unruly and believes the root of misery to be the truth and protects it.

The ātmā is ageless and immortal. Believe it to be your true form, beyond the body, and daily contemplate on this fundamental truth. The bliss of the ātmā is like nectar and the happiness of the body is like poison. The body disturbs the mind. Constantly remain aware of this.

In the Arab world, the oil was always there. They lived and walked on top of it, but they did not know that there was oil 10,000 feet beneath their feet. Any precious thing is to be found deep down. Gold, pearls or diamonds are all found deep down. Likewise, the soul is deep within us. Here today, in India, we export spirituality and import rubbish! (Smirking and smiling) East goes West and the West goes East!

ME: The ātmā is immortal, right? But how many ātmās are there? Do they multiply?

KESHAV: Each individual ātmā is unique. After ultimate redemption, it no longer travels through the cycles of birth and death. But as to how many there are... well, there are innumerable... there's simply no way of counting.

We must go back to the original ancient wisdom, without which we won't become happy, regardless of how much comfort or external progress we may have. In 1986, we went to Germany and we visited the Mercedes factory. We saw the '86 model with the new airbag system. It was the first car at the time. We were impressed, but they told us that they still had 90 percent improvement left to make. Then another swami with us asked: "Who causes the most accidents – the car or the driver?" (chuckling) You've seen all these signs and sayings right? Don't Drink and Drive. You drive like hell and you'll soon be there! Improvements don't need to always be made in the cars, but in the minds of the drivers too! If you get it, you'll understand...

सुखम्
Sukh
[soo-kha]
happiness; joy

We live in an age of hyper-individualism. We live in an age of promotions, presentations and perceptions. The meaning of truth, peace and harmony constantly changes. Showmen succeed and real men fail. There are more peace conferences today than ever before, yet the budget for military and armed forces rises for every nation, every year. We have more motivational books, podcasts and speakers than ever before, yet the most foolproof industry is that of drugs. We live in an age where we glorify ideas and utopian visions, but we never try to emulate those very ideas.

ME: Why aren't we happy as a society?

KESHAV: We live in a delusion. That is the cause of misery. We are running after the wrong things because of this very delusion. Many think that the more money they have, the happier they will be, but this is a delusion. Happiness is not proportionate to how much money one has – ever (shaking his head). This is straight practical application. There is no need to think or ponder upon it, it is based on the experience of millions. We see it all around us. People may appear happy externally, but in reality, no matter how much one tries to hide it, people have many problems.

The average man today has more comfort than any of the emperors of the past, yet we still remain unfulfilled. Why? Because everyone has it. That is why we're not emperors! Comparisons. Inclusiveness. In the culture of individualism, it seems to hurt us. Happiness is elusive. The moment we think we get it, we want something else. Where do we look for happiness? Power? Napoleon had half the world under his feet when he said that he had not seen six happy days in his life! Fame? Michael Jackson, one of the most followed and loved singers of all time, at the peak of his career said that it hurts to be him. Charlie Chaplin said, "I could make the whole world laugh, but even if the whole world came together, they couldn't make me laugh."

ME: But it's okay to make money and strive for success in such a way?

KESHAV: It depends. We need money, of course, we live in society and we need to thrive and survive. But to believe that the more money you will have, the happier you will be is wrong. Don't be deluded. Externally, it may appear that one who has money is happy, but no matter how much money one accumulates, it will only create unhappiness. Maharaj says: "Wealth is regarded as even greater than the body. The body is readily sacrificed, but wealth is not readily given up."

I went to someone's home in the USA once and there was a 14 x 14 basement for storing gold and valuable items. I asked the owner if they had it made themselves. He told me that the previous owner must have, because when they brought the property it was already there. The space could have been enough to house at least 2000kg of gold! It was a steel-walled basement! Impossible to even penetrate! Now, doesn't it make you wonder that if someone had so much gold and valuable items, what made them sell their home? I later found out that they had gambled away all their money! It's not about not making money. It's about discipline. If you command your wealth, you are free and rich. If your wealth commands you, you are poor indeed. Whatever one achieves immorally will be a source of pain and misery. Intention matters. Money is known as artha. If one doesn't know how to use it, then it becomes anartha (misfortune). Dharma *must* come first. It's the foundation of the four endeavours of human life. Artha comes after. Dharma is the brake, and artha is the accelerator. Now, would you purchase a car without a brake? Then why do we do it in life?

Look at how many people commit suicide daily! I once came across a book in France on ways to take one's own life! And when we look at the history of those who commit suicide, they usually come from a comfortable and educated background. So, the problem isn't in a lack of something external, but internal. The problem is in the mind. Humans crave power, intelligence, fame, etc. – but none of this will give happiness. It is all an illusion. This is a fact.

ME: Happiness depends on the condition of my mind?

KESHAV: Exactly. Everything outside may be well set, but inside we can still be upset. The saying goes: 'asthir man dukh, sthir man sukh' (an unstable mind brings misery, a stable mind brings happiness). You may have everything, but without a stable mind, you will not be happy.

All problems are of the mind. There is little external influence on the problems themselves. It all depends on perspective. To you, one person can look like an enemy, but to another he could be a friend. Everything is a reflection of your mind. As you see, so you are. Nothing causes happiness or misery outside of the mind. Everyone thinks that the more they have – the more comfort they have – the more happy they will be. This is a misunderstanding. To a certain degree it may help, but it's not that the more you have, the more happy you will be. Happiness and misery are both concepts of the mind. The solution to all problems are to be resolved in the mind too.

ME: How does the mind become stable?

KESHAV: Through the knowledge of the ātmā and Paramātmā (the supreme being) and samjan (spiritual understanding). The more you try to search for happiness in your own way, the less you will find it. The modern approach is wrong, it is centred around individualism and is body-conscious. We do everything for our bodies, but not for what's inside! Comfort and happiness are two different things. We think that comfort is happiness and so we suffer. It is our mind that is unstable and polluted. When one experiences inner joy and remains stable, no matter how much turbulence arises externally, it can be said that they have developed complete faith in God and Guru.

ME: You said earlier that the mind is both the cause of happiness and misery, or something along those lines?

KESHAV: (nodding) Yes. All the fights in the world stem from a polluted mind. If the mind is pure, there would be no wars. The pollution within needs resolving before the pollution outside. What is inside is more important than what is outside. We cannot see mental pollution, but unfortunately, it harms us the most. So, the more we go 'in', the more 'one' things become. All swabhavs (base natures) are rooted in the mind.

First, man fought by hand, then by stones, bow and arrows, then iron weapons, then guns and bombs, and now the nuclear bomb! What's next?! Humanity has changed everything outside but has failed to make the most significant change needed – the one within one's own mind. If everyone's mind became pure, heaven would be right here on earth. William James said: "The greatest discovery of our generation is that human beings can alter their lives by altering the attitudes of the mind."

ME: Aren't there numerous causes for wars and differences of opinions? Surely everyone is just searching for happiness? Not that this justifies any of that...

KESHAV: The only difference between every individual on this planet is their skin. Take that away and everything is just flesh, blood and bone. The cause of all wars and differences of opinion is *this*. If everyone realises themselves to be the ātmā, and is able to disidentify with the body, there would be no differences or fights. After purifying one's mind and realising the ātmā, there is nothing more left to be done. After that, there is only infinite bliss and happiness.

A devotee by the name of Rajbai asked Maharaj: "If you are truly happy upon us, what happens?" Maharaj told her: "I will make you flawless. You have become mine, so I do not wish to leave a single flaw in you." The peace of God and the ātmā supersedes all other pleasures. Shri Krishna says: "For one who never unites the mind with God there is no peace; and how can one who lacks peace be happy?"[1] This form of happiness comes from patience and faith.

ME: Is misery just a part of life?

KESHAV: All of creation has laws. Most of creation lives within the laws. Only humans wish to seek 'total freedom'. Then, we are the ones who want to complain that we face misery and unhappiness in life! When we don't live within dharma (righteous conduct), there is nothing but misery and suffering. If you live within dharma, you develop the samjan around suffering and rise above it. There is always more misery than happiness in the worldly pleasures.

The ancient scriptures say that the body is the home of happiness and sorrow. Pramukh Swami used to say that sansār[2] is full of miseries and more miseries! The desire for money, worldly gain, honour, and glory for the individual brings unhappiness. Misery will come. Pain will come. I won't lie to you and say they won't. It is the way of the

---

[1] Bhagavad Gita 2.66
[2] life in this realm

world. But we should develop the strength to tolerate. If you attain the knowledge of ātmā and Paramātmā, why would you ever become dejected? Happiness and misery is based on prārabdha[3]. That is why no matter what difficulties or situations you face, you should not allow them to touch your heart. If you develop such wisdom, you will rise above suffering.

We experience even more misery because of the way society is shaped today. Our body is a slave to our desires, so it is then clear that difficulties will arise. Even the true devotees have had tough times, but they remained unaffected because they had understanding. Even Muktanand Swami suffered from tuberculosis! Know that the body is the home of disease. Misery will come and go, but we should dispel it with understanding. The Guru gives us such understanding. We cannot dispel misery by our own means or comprehension. On the path of dharma, there are hundreds of obstacles. They are overcome through wisdom. We should stand up to and fight difficulties. Don't give in. Don't become disheartened.

ME: Is there any past occurrence which, when comes to mind, upsets you?

KESHAV: (laughing) Unhappiness is forgetting the Guru and the coming to one's mind of thoughts other than that of God. I have had no such problems. I constantly experience bliss and only more bliss.

---

[3] karmic deeds whose consequences are already set in motion

ME: What causes the mind to become weak, and for us to repeatedly face misery?

KESHAV: When reality doesn't meet expectations. When we don't get things the way we want. This is the biggest influence on human unhappiness. If we suffer a loss, grief, or the like, we become unhappy, dejected, or full of misery. Some even experience depression or suicidal thoughts. Life is the way it is. Acceptance is key. We should never blame another individual, circumstances, or a situation for the way we feel. It will *never* help. What happens to you is only 10 percent, how you react to it is 90 percent. Happiness and misery is based on nothing more than your own reactions.

In the Gita, Shri Krishna says: "The sense objects recede for a person who abstains from indulging in them. However, the longing for them does not subside. The longing subsides [only] when one's vision reaches [i.e. realises] the transcendental [i.e. God]."[4] Indulgence in pleasures only leads to more misery. Maharaj has said that as long as there is a desire for worldly pleasures, divine bliss is not attained.

This temporary body is so dependent, the jiva develops false attachment to it and suffers. Happiness is attained according to one's nature. Happiness and misery are experienced due to the association with the material body. One who realises the exact form of their own ātmā and develops the true knowledge of Paramātmā, perceives the association of the body and the world like a dream [i.e. temporary]. Maharaj says that

---

[4] Bhagavad Gita 2.59

as long as one sees happiness in worldly objects, one's mind is like that of an animal. The ancient scriptures say that our innate nature is happiness. Sat (truth), chitt (consciousness), ānand (bliss) is the very nature of the ātmā. If we go back to this innate nature, we experience happiness. In [Vachanamrut] Loya 10, Maharaj says: "One should believe, 'I am the ātmā – pure, full of consciousness, unchanging, the embodiment of bliss and imperishable.' He only believes his own self, the ātmā, to be the embodiment of bliss, viewing other objects to be insignificant, perishable, inert and full of unhappiness. He believes that any happiness apparent in the worldly pleasures is only due to the ātmā's presence in the body. But, when the ātmā leaves the body, everything becomes inert and full of misery."

ME: So, happiness is a choice that we can constantly make?

KESHAV: No individual or situation, in and of itself, can make you unhappy if you choose not to let it. If you are unhappy, it is likely the fault of your mind. If not the fault, then the call to action is always with you and you alone. Our instant reaction is to push the blame onto someone or something else, whereas the scriptures tell us that no one in this world, or no situation in this world, can make us act wrongly or behave wrongly if we do not want it to be so.

Nelson Mandela suffered a lot in his life, primarily because of John Foster, who wanted to keep him in prison as long as possible. When Mandela was released, he was asked what he thought of John Foster. Mandela simply said: "He is a decent man." Mandela had the heart to forgive. He put the past behind him, and because of that, South Africa exists today. Look at his mental attitude. He *chose* happiness. He *chose* to forgive. When terrorists attacked Gandhinagar Akshardham, Pramukh Swami *never* asked the names of the perpetrators. Instead, he prayed that no one be misguided to commit such acts in no religion, no place, nowhere in the world. Look at this attitude! Kalam didn't say that Pramukh Swami taught him how to transcend 'I' and 'me' for no reason! If you are stable from within, nothing will affect you. When one develops their character, there is nothing but peace and happiness in life.

ME: What is the true source of happiness?

KESHAV: Tulsidas, the author of the Ramayan, wrote from his own experience: "There is no happiness in the heavens, on earth, or even in the nether regions; bliss lies only at the feet of God or his holy Sādhu." He even says in the Ramayan that there is no happiness in this perishable world. Realising *this* is the first step.

Gunatitanand Swami said: "All the joys of this world are always rooted in misery."[5] Realise that none of the worldly pleasures will bring happiness to the jiva. Wealth and worldly objects may give joy to the body temporarily, but the ātmā experiences bliss in a different way.

---

[5] Swamini Vato 1/101

God is the source of all happiness. Nothing else exceeds such happiness. When we truly understand this, we can remain stable in any crisis. Maharaj says: "Joy and sorrow are intertwined, but remain strong and stable-minded." Happiness and misery are intertwined. They are relentless. Refuge in God is the solution to all problems. First, understand God to be the all-doer. Then, seek refuge in God. We often lack this faith. But with this understanding, nothing can affect you.

If happiness was to be found in wealth and fame, then would it not give us inner joy and peace? Then why are, those with either depressed, lonely, sad, or taking their lives? Some even need sleeping pills! Money may buy big mansions and a comfy bed, but only the thought of God will grant sound sleep. God has given us this human body, and yes, living in this world we do have social obligations. You earn money to buy a home, provide for a family among other things, but remember that the foundation of all bliss and happiness is God.

God is true. Mandirs are true. The scriptures are true. By accepting and living by their principles, one can experience true happiness and peace. Gunatitanand Swami also said that if you want to remain happy, think of those who are worse off than you.[6] Muktanand Swami writes: "Even kings are unhappy, the poor are unhappy, and the wealthy are also unhappy. Without discretion, even monks remain unhappy... In this world, only the Sant is truly happy." Pramukh Swami once said: "We have not come to

---

[6] Swamini Vato 4/83

see the country. We have come to convey the message of God, to teach the noble way of righteousness and lead them onto the path of true happiness."

ME: Is it because I have desires that I remain unhappy?

KESHAV: You may be able to renounce the world, but desires are even more difficult to renounce. Only one with no desires is truly happy. Life is full of ups and downs, joys and miseries. In times of difficulty, we become mentally disturbed. Only by firm conviction and refuge in God do we attain peace and happiness. People blindly crave for more and more wealth and power. This is the human struggle. For this, some don't even care through what means they achieve them. It is not wrong to acquire either, but it must be done so abiding by dharma. Honest effort – purushārth – is the first requirement. Establish dharma in one's life and then set out on all endeavours. In this way, you will become happy and experience peace.

If one lives a pure and noble life, everything else will follow. Even if one has a lot of wealth, but if he lacks positive virtues, he will only fall into misery. You must also learn to live simply. Living simply is the key to happiness. Do not become extravagant. The main thing is that one's life must be pure. Where there is moha (infatuation), there is no happiness. Today, everyone in this world is a prisoner of moha, and that is why people remain unhappy.

ME: What is that moha?

KESHAV: It is to believe what is false (perishable) as true (permanent), and what is true as false. All worldly objects we attach ourselves to are perishable. We do everything for the body, but in the end it perishes. It isn't immortal. Whatever happiness is described for worldly pleasures does not, in fact, exist forever. All of one's efforts are wasted in the pursuit of worldly pleasures. The indulgence in the pleasures of the world is believed to be the source of happiness, and so, everyone chases after worldly joys. But it is like a mirage, in which, as one approaches it, it only goes further away. Exposure to outer objects of pleasure overpowers even the most resolute.

ME: So ultimately it is God that is the source of all happiness?

KESHAV: Yes, that's right. Kabir says: "Cast stones at those pleasures through which God is forgotten." If we indulge in worldly pleasures, God leaves our heart. He then says: "Be pleased with such sorrows that allow us to continuously recite God's name."

Once a fifty-storey building needed to be painted. To climb and hang from a fifty-storey building is daunting and difficult in itself! The painters had forgotten to bring their brushes, so they started throwing coins from above [to draw attention to themselves]. No one looked up. People passing by would simply put the money in their pockets and continue walking. All the painters' coins soon ran out. They then started throwing pebbles down from the stonework. Although they removed eight to ten pebbles, only one was needed. When they threw the pebble, a passer-by was hit on the head and he looked up! Similarly, when God showers us with money, wealth and pleasures, no one looks towards him. But when God puts a pebble or an obstacle in our way, only then do we look towards him.

ME: But why do we have to face obstacles in life to attain happiness?

KESHAV: The obstacles we face allow us to remain close to God. If we take it positively, then nothing remains to be done. We think God doesn't look towards us. In reality, it is only because God looks towards us that we are able to do anything at all!

Nishkulanand Swami writes: "Never grant us those pleasures from which sorrows arise. Always give us those difficulties through which we experience happiness." Whatever difficulties come our way, tolerate them and move forward. Through them we should constantly remember God and let it be. We shouldn't accept pleasures through which God is forgotten. If we take it positively, then our work here is complete.

Throughout life, we may face various issues such as recession, disease, grief, or anything for that matter, but that is so that we don't become too attached *here*. God may send many such difficulties our way so that we don't become stuck here. There is no need to despair or panic. Keep a calm mind. Let the thoughts pass. Stay positive.

Maharaj has said: "In times of difficulties, one should remain patient. Everyone's life is in the hands of God." Happiness and misery are like a cloud cover, they are not in one's control. Yogi Bapa used to say that the pleasures of this world are like a baby's dummy. Babies suck on dummies but they don't get real milk from them. We have been served real milk [in the form of spirituality]. So why should we despair?

Whatever God does is always for the best. Remain content. God has gone to the extent of reducing the pain of death to that of a thorn prick! God wants to give us ultimate, permanent happiness and peace. Therefore, let him do whatever is necessary. Never wallow in self-pity. If you do wallow, misery will never be overcome. Understand and accept these words to be the ultimate truth. Only then will you feel at peace.

Those who trust God remain happy even in the times of hardship. This is not understood by those with the opposite understanding. The more the mind ignores this, the more misery one endures. The Pandavas trusted God, so their glory is sung till this day and Shri Krishna kept their side! Everything that has evolved from māyā is perishable.

Maharaj says that the difference between material and divine happiness is like that of day and night. Material happiness is temporary. All miseries reside in indulgence of the senses. In all truthfulness, the soul craves divine happiness, not the temporary happiness that we indulge in.

ME: But the mind is constantly drawn towards worldly pleasures!

KESHAV: That's because the seeds of such pleasures are rooted in your mind. The more spiritually inclined you become, the more you learn and gain knowledge, and the more your mind is subdued. If you see someone attractive, don't you feel you are naturally drawn towards them? But if you have knowledge, you can restrain your mind.

The essence of whatever texts the leaders of countless different beliefs have created is to break one's bondage to sense pleasures. The indulgence of the senses is the root of all misery. If the desire to indulge in pleasures is overcome, all miseries will be overcome. Just as adding ghee (clarified butter) and wood further fuels a fire, indulging in sense pleasures only increases our desire for them.

ME: The scriptures tell us, and so do our experiences in life, that the the bliss of God is greater than the pleasures of the world. You mentioned this too. However, we are still attached. How do we stop this?

KESHAV: Despite being aware of the deficiency, we are still attracted to them because our conviction of the deficiency is not total. For example, we know that poison is deadly, so we never feel like taking it. If we have a similar conviction here, we will never be attracted towards them. That is, if we want liberation... 'vishayan vishavat tyajet' (the pleasures of this world should be discarded like poison).

ME: Though you say that, and even if I agree... as soon as I leave your vicinity, I will still feel like enjoying them. I don't experience constant happiness either way. Why?

KESHAV: That is because we tend to have a passion for sense pleasures. This actually stems from a desire of the soul. When we become miserable, we feel that such passion is wrong, but deep down we don't believe it. We become agitated because of our own ignorance. By not following the spiritual commands, we experience unease. To control the mind, we have to strengthen the belief in our ātmā. The more we engage in satsang, the more firm it becomes. First, you must realise that this world consists of nothing but pain and misery; it is false and temporary. Secondly, understand that God is eternal and true. We haven't understood this. When we study, we don't simply acquire all the knowledge at once, but the more diligently we study, the more we learn. The same applies with satsang.

ME: There are so many attractions and temptations around us today. How do we control the senses? Also, you travel all over the world, but you are able to maintain so much discipline in your life... How?

KESHAV: (laughing and shaking his head) There will be temptations wherever you go. If we want to keep control, we should keep our eyes on āgnā (spiritual commands). We are devotees. We have a Guru. We must have complete faith, trust and conviction in what they tell us and teach us. We should never sway away from dharma-niyam (righteous conduct and spiritual commands). Remember, desires will never be fulfilled through indulgence. We shouldn't indulge in everything we get either. Poison is made for some uses, but we discriminate and stay away from it. Fire has been created for us to use but we don't put it in our mouths, do we?

ME: Is there even such a thing as everlasting bliss here on earth?

KESHAV: You can see it in the lives of great devotees like Narsinh Mehta, Mirabai, or Dada Khachar. They constantly remained positive and situated in bliss. Did they ever feel dejected or depressed? They understood that worldly problems come and go, so why should they affect us? Engage in bhakti and remain cheerful. People like Virchand Modi, Dr. Bajadia, Upendrabhai, that youth from Canada – they had understanding, so they experienced constant bliss, regardless of their personal circumstances. The world may label such individuals as mad, but one who has such joys will never experience misery. One who has bhakti (devotion) and mahimā (understanding of greatness) always remains joyful and happy.

Happiness alone is never experienced. Difficulties will always arise. Time changes. Just like the layers of the earth are all different, similarly, situations in our life are different and constantly subject to change. Material objects are easily gained, and they are just as easily lost. But the bliss of God and Guru is everlasting. I continuously pray that all may experience this happiness and develop the understanding to do so...

Swabhav

[swuh-bhaa-va]

base nature, temperament, or inner instincts

Human nature affects every individual on this planet. We are all a slave to our base natures and instincts. The Sanskrit word 'swabhāv' means 'base nature', 'temperament', or simply, 'human nature'. At the deepest level of our existence, we know that our nature is often the cause of most of our misery, but we are unable to get to grips with it. Pramukh Swami once said: "In developing externally, we also have to develop just as much internally, so that the difficulties that exist today between people – bias and dislike, partiality of 'mine and 'yours', etc. – all disappear. We have to remove *all* the faults within us and attain virtues."

Psychologists describe the rewards of personal comfort, the sexual urge and the striving for appreciation and superiority as the three fundamental forces behind all human behaviour. They determine creativity, planning, decision-making and goal-setting. To be above these forces is to be above human behaviour. It is to be divine.

The Greek philosopher Socrates is quoted by Plato in his work *Xenophon Memorabilia*: "Having the fewest wants, I am nearest the gods… My belief is that to have no wants is divine." Bhagwan Shri Swaminarayan also proposed that all souls are enveloped by the eternal ignorance of māyā or vāsanā (desires). Vāsanā is principally greed for wealth, mutual attraction between men and women, and the craving for ego. One who is above all forms of ignorance is divine.

KESHAV: The cause of misery and disturbances is one's own nature. It is the *only* thing that troubles us. These base natures are embedded deep within our minds. The scriptures say: 'man eva manushyānām kāranam bandha mokshayoho' (the mind is the cause of both bondage and liberation of man). It is the mind that, through the base instincts, creates troubles. The mind gets all types of thoughts about whether it should do something or not. The mind *must* be conquered. When the mind becomes idle, it engages in negative thoughts, actions and decisions.

It is only through improving and elevating one's own character that a human being becomes good — not by money, fame, or intelligence. Man is known by his character. If one has purified their character, there are no issues. Maharaj has said that the fruit of spirituality is to purify one's nature. One's demeanour or virtuous personal behaviour is also the key to inspiring others towards noble thoughts and actions.

ME: Are you saying that the cause of *all* misery is our nature?

KESHAV: Yes. In Vasai, near Ahmedabad, there were two brothers. One was sleeping on his cart, blocking the road outside their home, and the younger one wanted to pass with his vehicle. He called out to his brother to move his cart slightly so he could pass. The brother, half-asleep, said: "I am not waking up or moving!" The younger brother got angry, picked up a rock, and smashed his brother's head in with it. He was jailed. Nature. This is a true story, and I'm sure you've heard many such stories, but it's up to us to understand. Our base natures are so dangerous that they can even make us destroy those we love most. They are like inner shadows and demons that need to be overcome. When base natures are overcome, bliss is to be experienced right here. The root of unhappiness is our base natures. It is the root of all war and conflict, and we fall into the trap again and again, generation after generation.

ME: What are the base natures?

KESHAV: One's behaviours are one's nature. They are the likes of lust, anger, greed, avarice, infatuation, egotism, jealousy, fear, and grief. They afflict every human being on this planet. All of the base natures need to be destroyed to experience true bliss and joy. All base natures are rooted in body-consciousness. We are a bundle of our natures. Worldly pleasures consist principally of wealth [i.e. greed], lust and ego. All the misery, destruction and unease that you see around you is all due to the base natures. Nothing external needs to be changed as such. The only thing we need to change is our attitude and intent. It is our base instincts which hinder all spiritual progress and blind us in illusions.

ME: It seems like such a difficult task to get rid of my swabhāvs. It will probably take a lifetime! What should I do?

KESHAV: That is up to you. Believe them to be your real enemies.

EGO

We fear letting go of the 'I' that is so doggedly deep rooted in humanity's conscience. To erase one's ego seems like we're melting the self away. Modern society teaches egocentricity from birth. The cuddly newborn baby in every home becomes the centre of attraction. When the baby smiles, the whole family smiles with it; when it cries, all try their best to appease it. Enjoying this form of undivided love and attention, the baby quickly learns how to get its way. As they grow older, every child craves for that same undivided attention. In this way, man grows into a creature addicted to his own ego. He is satisfied only when he expresses his individuality, and when his existence is appreciated. Humility then becomes a dispensable, redundant, and often, unnecessary option in life.

In Vachanamrut Jetalpur 1, Maharaj reveals: "In the beginning, when no one honours a person, imagine what his nature is like. Then, when a hundred people begin to follow him, his self-conceit assumes a different type. Further, when a thousand people or a hundred thousand people follow him, or 10 million people follow him, his self-conceit becomes of a different type altogether." Many are modest, but on closer inspection one finds that a trace of personal gain, a tinge of fear, a hunger for praise, or a bad upbringing with humiliation has become the norm. In short, egotism inflates in proportion to the praise and position one receives within society, tribes and groups. Saint Bernard remarks: "It is not a great thing to be humble when you are brought low;

but to be humble when you are praised is a great and rare attainment." The English writer, John Ruskin, said: "The first test of a truly great man is his humility."

ME: And the ego is the worst of our natures?

KESHAV: It is. The ego is the root cause of all negativity. Muktanand Swami says that all spiritual endeavours are destroyed by the ego. We are *owned* by our ego. The need to fuel our ego ruins everything. Brahmanand Swami says: "Forsake the ego and drink the nectar of immortality through the Sant." Individuality is actually egotism. Absence of individuality means the total absence of ego. Muktanand Swami writes: "Erase the 'I' and God is near..." Thus, the total absence of ego denotes the total presence of divinity. It is the total manifestation of God.

No individual or circumstance in this world is responsible for your happiness other than your own nature. *That* nature stems from your mind. Obstinacy, ego and jealousy – these three are the worst natures, and all of them are rooted in body-consciousness. By letting go of 'I' and 'mine', you let go of all your base natures.

ME: What's wrong with having an ego?

KESHAV: Maharaj said that the ego ruins all endeavours. The ego is always attached to us wherever we go. One who is egotistical is demonic. The ego is a great enemy, as it fuels all the other base natures. Eighty percent of our ruin is from the ego, only 20 percent is from the other natures. It was King Parikshit's ego that made him throw the dead snake on the sage!

Tulsidas says: "Renounced he has women, wealth and possessions, but man lives on praises alone, the greatest of all obsessions." Tulsidas understood the addiction that man has to ego and the self. Maharaj himself dislikes ego. He dislikes sevā offered by egotistical people, referring to such people as being cunning and like a dog. This flaw of ego remained even in those considered great, because without spiritual understanding, one cannot let go of their ego. Some people are extremely self-centred, egotistic and arrogant, yet where they see self-benefit, they behave humbly – this is just as wrong!

Ego is a sweet poison and until you have an ego, you will never progress spiritually. All flaws arise from the ego. It emerges from ignorance and takes one into darkness. Ignorance itself is the root of ego. Yogi Bapa used to say: "Don't go down the path of taking poison!" We feel that in today's society we need an ego to establish our identity, but why? Maharaj went as far as saying that without the ego, everything seems tasteless to man.

The ego is the gravest of all sins and the biggest of all blemishes. One sees one's appearance as it is in a mirror. If one attributes faults to the mirror that is sheer ignorance. The more the ego, the more the actual insignificance. The greater the humility, the more the true greatness. Read [Vachanamrut] Vartal 11. Ego is the source of anger, envy and jealousy. One who is egotistical is like a demon. At some time or another, due to this ego, one will think they are above and beyond everyone else. Egotism is the gravest of all sins. When one sees everyone and everything as divine, the ego is eradicated. This is the master key. This is satsang.

ME: How do we conquer the ego?

KESHAV: Through dāsatvabhāv (radical humility). Muktanand Swami says: 'sab gun puran param viveki, gun ko mān na āve' (even one who is complete with all virtues, and has the highest level of discretion, should never become arrogant of his virtues). Yogi Bapa used to say that praise works magic on the ears! If we are praised or someone sings our virtues, even then we should remain humble. Never keep any form of I-ness or my-ness.

Kabir writes: "Everyone walks upright thanks to their ego, but nobody is able to walk low with humility. However, one who walks low with humility, he is the greatest of all." If one has an ego that 'I am the doer', it will lead to one's downfall, but if we believe God to be the all-doer, we can easily overcome the ego. Whatever God does is for our best. This thought should be predominant in one's mind.

ME: If we remain meek in this way, won't people take advantage of us? Isn't it a sort of dilemma?

KESHAV: In society, you shouldn't remain meek; remain authoritative. If someone challenges you, answer them in appropriate manner, but always speak with respect. On the spiritual path, you should always behave with radical humility. No two people are the same. Always keep this in mind when dealing with conflict.

So long as there is ego, one does not develop detachment. So long as there is ego, one will never develop any positive qualities. That is what Yogi Bapa said. If you wallow in self-pity, your mind will never experience peace. One who tolerates is humble. No one has tolerated like Bhagatji. There is no one comparable to him.

ME: Why and how should I cultivate humility in life?

KESHAV: One who bows is bowed to by all. However, if you remain stubborn due to your ego, others will also remain stubborn too. You may think that you are great, but for others you are fake! One who isn't humble is liked by none. Humility is a safety zone. No questions or problems remain for one who cultivates complete humility.

You develop this form of humility by serving the Guru with total servitude (dāsānū dās) more than by any other spiritual means. On the spiritual path, you must learn to bow down to others and not make others bow down to you. Understand others to be greater than you, reduce yourself to the insignificant.

By having the single virtue of humility all other virtues are bestowed upon you. It is our arrogance that distorts our inclinations and thoughts, but when one practices satsang humbly, one progresses further and further. Greatness is of no importance when it is devoid of humility. One who is not humble cannot be great. The fruits of innumerable types of knowledge lie in humility. Knowledge coupled with humility shines.

One who is affected by praise and insult is extremely raw. However, one who remains humble amidst either extreme is ripe. One who talks humbly possesses power, because humility is the power of God. Humility is a binding force. On attaining it, all of our batteries remain bound and packed together. Without humility, all virtues exit one after the other, and life becomes empty and barren.

There is nothing greater than humility. Humility is God's virtue. It is the father of all virtues. The seed of all virtues lies in humility. If one does not have humility, then whatever virtues one has will trouble the individual. We don't like being humble! When we express humility, we often do so out of force [or because we have to], however, by becoming humble from within, we will attain God.

GREED, ENVY AND JEALOUSY

A Chinese proverb says: "Gold is tested by fire, a man by gold." Pramukh Swami and Mahant Swami pass that test categorically. Greed, envy and jealousy have failed to touch them. They have never been lured by the desire for wealth because they have no desires for material pleasures. The Bhagavad Gita says: "He who is unattached everywhere, who is not delighted at obtaining good or dejected at receiving bad, is poised in wisdom."[1] They personify the essence of the Moksha-Dharma canto of the Shānti Parva chapter in the Mahabharat: "In comparison to the bliss of God's abode, the pleasures of even the deities are deemed hellish."

ME: We are taught that greed is bad and that fulfilment lies in simplicity. Yet why do we find it difficult to put this into practice in our lives?

KESHAV: Because today, man's desires are forever increasing. We know that there is only discontent in the more we try to gain, yet we still run after it. It's nothing new though. Duryodhan said: "I know the path of dharma but cannot tread it. I know the path of evil, but I cannot shed it." We all know that conflicts are caused by greed, yet we can't stop ourselves. Look how people are killed in the quest for power and money. Yogi Bapa said the mind's nature is to keep desiring, so it is desires that we should kill!

---

[1] Bhagavad Gita 2.57

LUST, INFATUATION AND LAZINESS

The 18th century Irish poet and dramatist, Oscar Wilde, reveals the flaw of the great majority when he honestly admitted: "I can resist everything except temptation." How many of us relate? Lust really is an innate instinct of every living being – human or animal. To be untouched by lust is nothing but outright divinity.

The Guru is pratyaksh Nārāyanswarup – the manifest form of Narayan himself – unflinchingly established and attracted to God alone. It is for this very reason that Shri Krishna says: "Whatever action a great man performs, common men follow. Whatever standards they set by exemplary actions, the whole world pursues."[2]

ME: What about lust?

KESHAV: Brahmachārya is difficult to follow in its complete form [mentally] fully, but physically it *must* to be followed. Shri Krishna says: "One who wishes to achieve the highest liberation should practice celibacy."[3] It is one of the most fundamental teachings. It applies to one and all. Look at Pramukh Swami! He lived his life at the epitome of brahmachārya.

---

[2] Bhagavad Gita 3.21
[3] Bhagavad Gita 8.11

ME: The vow of non-lust is so difficult to follow in the modern world. What do we do?

KESHAV: Yes, that's an extremely difficult situation (chuckling). It wasn't like this before. But today, it is like 70 percent superficial [i.e. everyone wants to show off and present the best version of themselves] and only 30 percent reality. If you understand the greatness of satsang, you will have no trouble. But you cannot be lazy. Laziness and being laid-back is literally killing time and energy. Cleanliness is next to godliness. Maharaj has also said that we should control the desire for tasty foods. The more tastes we indulge in, the more the lust. Lust resides in the five types of taste: sweet, sour, salty, spicy and bitter. Food intake is to sustain the body, not to indulge.

Lust is uprooted when one imbibes dharma fully. The ego is dissolved when knowledge is fully realised. The strings of affection are cut when absolute detachment is acquired. The mind becomes free of taste and greed when one develops ekāntiki bhakti[4] coupled with an appreciation of God's greatness. Otherwise, the deficiencies of the base natures will never be overcome. Nor will there be any happiness in life, and one will die unfulfilled. There is no greater dignity in the entire cosmos than to observe the vow of non-lust. The misery of the cycle of birth and death reside in lust and ego, along with greed.

---

[4] single-minded devotion with dharma, (jnān) knowledge and vairāgya (non-attachment); the highest level of devotion

ME: Then what about love?

KESHAV: Love is highly subjective. Love for the body induces one to seek pleasures in worldly objects; that is kām (lust). Today, you will notice that the majority of the world strives to attain such pleasures. The scriptures say that if one can love the divine as one loves his body, in effect, diverting love from the body towards the divine, then even lust transforms into love.

ME: I regularly feel very lazy. I am not able to keep my mind set on tasks.

KESHAV: Laziness must be stamped out. If you keep a firm resolve that 'today's work must be completed today', then you will be able to accomplish your tasks. Never leave today's tasks till tomorrow. We should just put our heads down and get it done. You cannot afford this business of laziness in any of your activities – social, academical or spiritual.

FAULT-FINDING AND ANGER

ME: I constantly take abhāv-avgūn (finding flaws and faults) in others...

KESHAV: That is sweet poison. It feels good to begin with, but the trouble is only experienced later own. This is a personal deficiency. Don't give in so easily to such negative thought patterns. Yes, it is a flaw in the jiva itself, but the control is now on you. Even if someone else is speaking negatively about another person, stop them.

ME: Sometimes, words just come out, and we don't mean them – we later regret them. What then?

KESHAV: You must speak only when necessary. Silence is important. Pramukh Swami often used to say: 'maunāt sarvasiddhihi' (silence can accomplish everything). There is a saying I heard years ago, "End the day with a little quiet time; five or ten minutes alone with a worthwhile thought it makes your bed for you.

ME: Should I see faults in myself or view myself as perfect?

KESHAV: Your ātmā *is* perfect, but through the force of māyā and rebirths, the jiva is now associated with many flaws. Explaining [Vachanamrut] Panchala 3 to Pavitranand Swami, Bhagatji Maharaj said: "Until you see your own faults, you will not feel peace."

You should develop a habit of seeing your own flaws. It may seem controversial, but it is better than finding faults in others. By seeing faults in oneself, you can introspect and improve. That is the *only* thing within your own control. Even if someone says something to you, if you let it affect you, that is your own fault too. This is how Bhagatji thought.

We might develop externally, but we also have to develop just as much internally, so that the difficulties that exist today between people – bias and dislike, partiality of 'mine' and 'yours', polarisation, etc – all disappear. We have to remove all the faults within *us* alone and attain positive virtues.

ME: What is gossip?

KESHAV: Talking about others' fault, even when you don't know if it's true or not! This is khatpat (gossip), useless khatpat! When it isn't even true, it just makes it worse!

ME: I have long been a slave to my anger and ego. I want to be free of them...

KESHAV: Anger stems from ego. The ego is the root of all bad instincts. If you have self-pride and someone labels you as good or bad, what is your emotional state? Remember, we are neither very good or very bad. You do not become so upon someone saying this either. If you realise yourself as the ātmā, you are actually pure.

There is no place for anger or ego. We have to uproot such natures through knowledge. Also, if you can think 'everyone understands, only I don't understand', then who will you get angry upon? There is no doubt about it, your ego must be eradicated. It is because of self-pride that all conflicts arise. So forget your self-being. Whatever has been achieved is solely due to the grace of God.

CHARACTER, QUALITIES AND SPEECH

A statue of sentiments and a fountain of feelings, man is a highly emotional, unpredictable, yet still an intelligent creature. Each person is unique. We differ not merely by our physical appearances such as height, weight, skin colour, blood group or DNA, but also by our distinct and deferring minds. Emerson revealed: "It is a luxury to be understood." Lao Tzu said: "Sincere words are not grand." The tongue is also, in many ways, a second face. Pubilius Syrius, ironically a Latin writer of mimes says: "Speech is a mirror of the soul; as one speaks, so is he."

ME: What does it mean to win over the tongue?

KESHAV: If someone praises you, you don't become elated. If someone insults you, you don't become dejected. Know that as control over the tongue.

ME: I feel as though my swabhāvs affect me a lot. Sometimes I don't have the energy or ability to even try and overcome them. I become anxious and upset. I know I need spiritual wisdom at this point, but I just can't seem to do it.

KESHAV: You must have unflinching faith in God and Guru. They are here to rid us of our swabhāvs. We just need to maintain resolute faith. When it happens, it happens in a snap of their fingers. Continue with satsang and sevā. Live according to niyam-dharma. Brahmanand Swami asks Maharaj [in the Vachanamrut]: "We have attained the manifest God and satsang, but we still feel empty within, why is that?" Maharaj answered by saying that it is because one does not rely on the strength and faith of God and Guru.

If you rely on your own strength and faith, it won't last long. Of course, you need to make your own efforts, but ultimately, it is within their hands. Constantly fight your mind and swabhāvs like a boxing match! Personal efforts (purush-prayatna) and God's grace (ishwar krupā) – that is the formula. Never lose faith. Ever.

ME: Which qualities should we imbibe in our lives?

KESHAV: Honesty and integrity are of prime importance in one's life. If one has a pure character, all positive qualities automatically follow. One also becomes successful in life. By giving up character, you cannot hope to be successful, despite any efforts. Pramukh Swami said that even education without character destroys.

ME: Our mindset and attitude must play an important role, right?

KESHAV: Of course. If you put on yellow glasses, even a white wall will appear yellow. If you put on blue glasses, a white wall will appear blue. The glasses you wear will determine the colour you see. Likewise, how you are inside is how you will see and interact with the world around you. When Duryodhan was asked how he viewed everyone in the world, he said that everyone was useless, selfish, egocentric and bad. When Yudhisthir was asked how everyone was in the world, he said that everyone was virtuous, noble and good. One sees a glass as half-empty, another sees it as half-full, who is right?

ME: The one who sees the glass as half-full?

KESHAV: Both are right. The one who sees the glass as half-full is an optimist, the one who sees it as half-empty is a pessimist. Be the one who sees it as half-full. Cultivate positivity at all times, in all areas of life. Lincoln said: "He has a right to criticise who has a heart to help." Pramukh Swami had this nature. He was the purest being. When everyone was upset, he was set! He never let anything affect him throughout his life. He always adjusted. If you really think about it, nothing makes us unhappy as such, it all comes back to our own perception.

Your attitude determines how you will act. Your intent determines how you will act. No individual, circumstance, or external factor causes unhappiness or misery. It is only our own nature that causes us misery. The wise person learns this and is able to take things in a positive light. No matter what the circumstances, you can change how they affect you by changing your attitude.

Those you associate and surround yourself with also matter. Bad company comes also in the form of lust, anger, greed, attachment, desires, and other such flaws. So, whatever type of company one keeps, one's inner thoughts develop in that way, and thus, one acts in that manner. You should also shun the company of those who corrupt your character.

ME: What does it mean to be frank?

KESHAV: To be straightforward. What you are internally is what you should be externally. It also means to always be honest. This is how you will achieve success in all your endeavours.

ME: How do we overcome our swabhāvs and develop a pure character?

KESHAV: Through dharma. The refinement of sentiment is true progress. We change so much externally, but we don't do the same internally. Look at wars and conflict! Mankind has increased military power and weaponry, but why has no one thought about changing the mind? This is all sheer madness! No one thinks about this! Everybody's base nature is not the same. First, to recognise it is itself proper discretion. The best method to overcome swabhavs is to develop affection for the Satpurush. Niyam (codes of conduct) and nischay (resolute faith) reflect one's inner state. Man is known by the virtues he lives by.

In [Vachanamrut] Gadhada II-12, Maharaj gives a vivid analogy of the kingdom of the soul. The jiva (same as jivātmā) is said to be a true king only if it is able to control its subjects [i.e. the senses and the antahkarana]. A king rules his kingdom after he has read books on the art of ruling. He isn't subdued by pressure from his subjects and instead rules over them. However, if he has not learnt the art of ruling, people wouldn't obey his commands.

Similarly, if the jiva is weak, the senses will not allow it to rule. Therefore, those seeking liberation should not be weak in ruling the senses. They should develop their inner strength so that the senses and antahkarana remain obedient. This jiva is like a charioteer, the senses are like horses and the antahkarana is like the reins. One who knows how to hold and control the reins will never fall off. They will eventually achieve what they wish for. In this respect, if the jiva aspires to be a true charioteer, it must first train the mischievous senses, keep them in control, and make the antahkarana stable. This skill can only be learnt from the Satpurush.

Develop humility. In life, honour and insult should be accepted with equality. Neither are permanent, everything will go. Humility is like the digit '1', all other virtues are the '0's that may follow. As one's virtues increase, one becomes humble. It is a paradox of sorts. As long as there is life in this body, one should remain humble. Humility, patience and forgiveness are virtues beyond the three bodies and three states. The fruit of all knowledge is to remain humble before all.

The greater the humility, the more God's grace. There is nothing greater than humility. It is the king of all virtues. By remaining humble you defeat the ego. If you conquer your ego, you will automatically diminish body-consciousness and you will experience bliss and tranquility. All humans have a desire to become great, but without being humble towards all, real greatness is not attained. Maharaj says that there is no happiness in any worldly status, and that the fruit of acquiring innumerable types of knowledge is humility.

If you understand [Vachanamrut] Gadhada II-37, your swabhāvs will be destroyed. Without inner strength, your negative tendencies do not go. The mind is like a demon, never succumb to it. The mind is conquered by conquering the senses and base natures, which can only be eradicated by fighting with the mind as though it is one's enemy. If you conquer your mind, you conquer everything.

सेवा
Seva
[save-ah]
selfless service

The Roman philosopher, Cicero, said: "True glory takes deep root and spreads its branches wide, but all pretences soon fall to the ground like fragile flowers and nothing counterfeit can be lasting." Who we are in reality – our character – shines forth in the way that we serve others. Sevā has many facets, and here we focus on it in the wider sense of service towards God, Guru, and the community.

ME: What is the greatest endeavour?

KESHAV: To serve. A lot of people feel that service is a waste of time and energy, but this is not true. Normally, in society, service is often based on reciprocity, and so, nothing seems selfless. There is no purity of intention and that is why people see it as a loss. In the world, people serve others for their own selfish needs. Through spiritual endeavours, we serve selflessly. Nishkulanand says: "Sacrifice isn't about giving up rewards, it is about waiting for them patiently. Balance is key to a healthy life. To achieve this balance, find fulfilment through sacrifice rather than pleasure."

Great men perform sevā without any personal desires, praise, status, or comfort. Whatever sevā we get, we should seize the opportunity and do it. There should be no claims for particular sevā. Look at the discipline of the army! A captain's order is an order, and nobody questions it. When the 'leader' gives the command to do something, then you have to do it, without asking any questions.

Whatever we do, if we do it with the sole intent of pleasing God and Guru, then we will never feel unhappy. We should serve with love and enthusiasm. If you work as a security guard, you have to stand for eight hours. There are always two guards outside the Queen's palace (referring to Buckingham Palace). They aren't even allowed to move! Being accommodating towards all is a great form of service. Serving others is a form of devotion.

ME: Doesn't scientific research back up the benefits of volunteering and service?

KESHAV: (gently laughing) We don't tend to believe the ancient sages and scriptures, but we easily believe everything that science says. That is why everything needs to be backed up these days! This is just how society is now...

I once read an article in the Reader's Digest that presented research showing that doing good to people may be good for our heart, our immune system, and for all vitality too. Service is a form of medicine. Who knows, in the future, doctors may even prescribe service as a means to maintaining good health! There is lots of research. We could go into detail, but in short, service *only* has benefits when done with the purest of intentions.

Remember that all problems of the world are due to the human mind – whether that is individual or collective. It is through service that we develop stability of the mind, and through stability of the mind, we experience happiness and peace. Maharaj says: "One who is addicted to service overcomes all desires."[1] He also says: "All scriptures say one thing, do what makes God happy..."[2] That is sevā (service).

What matters most is your intent for engaging in sevā. You will never be able to satisfy the world, but if you satisfy God and Guru, you've satisfied everyone. Through service, you gain countless virtues. Everything else in this world is like rubbish! Put yourself into *this* 'garden'. Pramukh Swami said: "Never say 'do as much as you can', you can do as much as you will!" Intent is what matters. If you have the intent, you can do it.

Service to society, country, family and God is a necessary part of our lives. Service done with the motive for praise, money, or selfishness does not result in the progress of the country, peace at home, or in society. Nor does it reap the blessings of God and Guru. Only service that is selfless results in any real benefit.

ME: What is the best way to perform sevā?

KESHAV: The way Yogi Bapa said and did. By seeing nirdoshbuddhi (understanding of innocence and faultlessness) in one and all. This seems like brainwashing right? This isn't brainwashing – it's heartwashing! Nirdoshbuddhi is developed by purifying your

---

[1] Vachanamrut Gadhada 2.25
[2] Vachanamrut Gadhada 2.28

sentiments. Maharaj talks about Uddhavji in six Vachanamruts. Why? Because he saw nirdoshbuddhi in the gopis and their association with Shri Krishna. One should serve one's family, society, country, and God as long as there is life in this body.

The best way to perform sevā is to become the devotee of even the devotee. Don't look at what others are doing. What are you here to do, and what are you doing? One who serves while understanding the glory of others, and sees his own faults, is great.

In fact, the fruit of all spiritual endeavours – meditation, yoga, chanting, austerities, detachment, etc. – is that one believes themselves to be the servant of even the servant [and to act with radical humility]. The status of dās (servant) is the highest. To serve through mind, word and deed is greater than even behaving as the ātmā, according to Maharaj. Bhakti is itself sevā. Engage in bhakti with all your heart.

Out of the 273 Vachanamruts, 60 are about not looking at the flaws in others! Fault-finding are the snakes, seeing the positive virtues in others are the ladders. Look towards the ātmā – it is inherently divine, flawless and blissful.

The body is nothing, the ātmā is everything. This life isn't a game! To enjoy the inherent bliss of the ātmā and not see the flaws in others is true peace. To see everything and everyone as divine is itself moksha. Greatness is achieved through serving others.

The most difficult form of sevā is to fight one's mind. Break the mind into pieces. Keep persisting until that happens. Understand what needs to be done and just do it. That is the highest level of understanding. That is moksha in itself. Don't toil away all your life simply for worldly things. Everyone already does that. Engage in sevā too. That is the means to achieve divine grace.

Yogi Bapa used to say that one should be *addicted* to sevā, but it should never be done to inflate one's ego. Singing the praises of Tyagvallabh Swami, he once said: "Look at his humility and bhakti. He serves all. No anger. Always at peace. He never gets angry. He has sacrificed himself. To develop such humility is difficult." Fulfilment lies in becoming small. There is no greater peace than that which lies in servitude and humility. There is no higher dharma than sevā. Serve. Stay humble. Tolerate.

सद्विचार:

Sadvichar

[sud-vee-chaar]

positive thoughts and outlook

Adi Shankaracharya said: 'jitam jagat ken, mano hi yen' (one who conquers the mind, conquers the world). Plato said: "Self-conquest is the greatest of all conquests." A single person's attitude can change the world. In the Second World War, it was Churchill's attitude. The symbol of 'V' for victory and the words: "We will fight in the air... toil, sweat, blood and tears..." It is what made the British victorious. Victor Hugo said: "Bring on all the armies of the world. The attitude of a single man is more powerful than all the armies of the world." A positive attitude begins with positive thoughts.

ME: What is the importance of developing a positive mindset?

KESHAV: Shastriji Maharaj gave us the key to keeping an open mind. He said: "I never look at the negatives of anyone. I only focus on the positives." Yogi Bapa was at the pinnacle of positivity and open-mindedness. Today's world is such that we are so cushy in our comfort zones that we can't tolerate the smallest of adverse circumstances. In this way, our mind gets affected too. Science has shown that thinking negatively, or doing things to harm another, only harms our body and mind.

Yogi Bapa once told me that a senior monk beat him at least a hundred times. *At least!* When I told him we should tell people about this, and I even wrote a letter explaining the incidents, he made me rip it up and made me promise never to tell anyone! I am saying this now because it's important. These incidences only came out after Yogi

Bapa was no longer physically present. This is how much the Guru has tolerated. We tolerate nothing in comparison to them, and that is why we need not just a positive mindset, but an open mind too. So that we can forgive, forget and move forward.

Ten percent is what happens to you, and 90 percent is how you react to it. Life is like a mixed bag of chocolates – there'll be both good and bad. You cannot reach heaven without first passing through hell. It comes back to our character. Without character and morality as the foundation, you cannot develop a positive mindset, nor can you attain God. Character is the foundation. If character is kept firmly intact, the monument of life built upon it will remain unshakeable. If character is lost, the monument will soon tumble. Keep all your thoughts and actions pure. Just think about Pramukh Swami! What lies in a great person's heart is echoed through his speech and what he speaks, he follows accordingly.

ME: Sometimes we naturally speak negatively or gossip. Is this bad?

KESHAV: Negative talk is an addiction. We are immersed in it. We enjoy gossip, but we need to know our limits. We are wasting time idly! Instead, get involved in seva. If you do something selflessly for others, your mind instantly becomes lighter and you can even save yourself from psychosomatic disease! Look at the life of Pramukh Swami – total stability amidst praise and insult, regardless of any circumstance or situation – complete adjustment. Always.

There are four types of negative talkers: one does it and enjoys it, one doesn't do it and doesn't like it, one likes it but doesn't do it, and one doesn't like it but still does it. Have you ever thought about where you fall? We follow the crowd – we are so easily swayed in – and because others do it, we do it. You've gossiped countless times in your life, has it benefitted you in any way?

Negative talk is sugarcoated poison. Gunatitanand Swami said: "The words one hears is how one becomes." It is not just the words we hear, it is the words we speak too. The glass is both half-empty and half-full, it all depends on your perspective. Which perspective will you choose?

Never develop manthrā-vrutti (manthrā[1] mindset)! We have this attitude without any reason. In front of the Satpurush, we're not even like a virus, so why do we hold on to such a huge ego? Pramukh Swami has always pleased everyone – through his thought, word and deed. We can never compare ourselves to him.

You will become more unhappy if you continue to engage in gossip and fault-finding. It is unnecessary and futile! Instead, develop sādhu-vrutti (monk mindset). Maharaj says: "A true devotee never finds flaws in another *being*. One who finds flaws in others, never attains liberation."

---

[1] the servant of Queen Kaikeyi – step-mother of Shri Rama – in the Ramayan

We tend to cover our own mistakes and draw attention to those of others. We get so deluded that we try to prove this sort of view to ourselves too! To see one's own flaws and work on them is a high level of spirituality. Yogi Bapa said: "To see one's own flaws is the same as seeing God." The more bad you see in another, the more it will become a part of you. Whatever good you see in others, will be absorbed by you. Those who a truly virtuous always see the good in others. If you can't find your own faults then pray, think about God and Guru's commands, and compare one's life to that of the Satpurush.

Never speak or write words which will cause anyone harm or distress. One who sees flaws in another has a demonic jiva. Don't see anyone's flaws. Yogi Bapa said: "Close that road! Only see one's own flaws." Even to keep it in one's mind is abhāv (fault-finding). We must get to the root of negativity. Like Shakespeare said in Caesar: "Nip them in the bud." Get rid of this nature from the very root. To belittle is to be little. If you put other down, you come down too.

Words are the most powerful drug used by mankind. How you speak to others, particularly children, has a huge impact. I once read a book titled *Mind as Healer, Mind as Slayer.* Have a look at it. Your mind is the most powerful tool, it depends on how you use it. So be strong and brave. Never utter loose talks. Do not criticise or find faults in others. Whosoever perceives others as divine is indeed the most fortunate.

ME: But what if it is other people causing me to think negative?

KESHAV: No one makes you think negative except for your own mind! Stop looking towards others, and look towards yourself. Gunatitanand Swami said: "Those who praise you will also cut your throat. However, you must behave equally in both these situations and not think ill of another." But if you find a fault in another, you will definitely bear the outcome. What outcome? Your intellect will become corrupt and you will constantly ruminate on bad thoughts.

ME: How do we tackle a negative attitude?

KESHAV: There are two ways to dissolve a negative attitude. The first is to cultivate the spirit of 'in the joy of others', and the other is to have nirdoshbuddhi (a pure, faultless and inherently innocent outlook) towards all. We become what we think of others. Thus, we must perceive all to be divine. One who perceives all to be divine is brave, whereas one who doesn't is a coward. If you seek the faults in yourself, then no trace of misery remains. One who sees virtues in others is regarded as the best of people by Maharaj. Taking the virtues of others is such a quality that it results in the attainment of the highest praise.

ME: I often feel that we serve people so much, yet all we get in return is criticism!

KESHAV: Such things are always bound to happen. Shri Krishna was God, yet people criticised him! There are always those who will speak against even the great and noble. Because people's minds are like crows, they are constantly on the lookout for a weakness or a wound to attack. Blessed are the pure in heart for they shall see God. One who maintains a good outlook on life, they will see the good. So keep doing what you do and don't worry about what people say.

ME: If it all comes back to the mind. What should we do?

KESHAV: The mind is constantly wavering. We need stability of mind. This is achieved through satsang. It takes at least twenty years of your life to finish your education. Likewise, one has to be patient on the spiritual path too. It isn't instant! Have faith and associate with satsang. Engage in positive and wholesome thoughts. If a negative thought arises, flush it out instantly, otherwise it will destroy you. However, once the mind becomes divine, no problems will affect you.

When the mind becomes pure and doesn't waver in misery or joy, one becomes happy. Total equanimity. Happiness does not live in external wealth or objects. Having a pure mind and heart is just as important as maintaining the body for good health. When one's mind becomes pure, one experiences joy and wonder in all activities and areas of life.

There are three types of mind [mindsets]: an ordinary mind that thinks and may not think [it does everything that comes its way], a divine mind that [inspires] good actions, and an evil mind that never thinks of good thoughts [it always thinks of spoiling things]. Engage your mind in thinking about what you have abundance of [spiritually]. How great God [whom I have attained] is and how insignificant am I in comparison? Isn't it astonishing that an ant can even meet an elephant! By developing this form of understanding, all tensions will be dissolved. Maharaj says: "Those who do not control the mind are not called human; they are like animals!"

The food you take in also matters. Maharaj says: "One's breath reflects what one eats. What one eats or drinks determines what one becomes within. Understand in the same way about visual, verbal, tactile and other sense pleasures." Through good intentions, the mind becomes good; through bad intentions, the mind becomes bad. A true identity is if one's visible actions are reflective of one's inner thoughts.

Of course, [outwardly] we have to fulfil out social duties and work. But, [inwardly] in our minds and hearts we should have love for God. A divine mind means to perceive positivity in all things. Also, having humility towards others, and glorifying the virtues of others, amounts to a divine mind. To remain stable amidst praise and insult is a great thing. The more one gives up one's ego, the more secure one becomes. An egoist will never ever experience true happiness! You *must* think positive. Don't ever think negatively! Those who adopt positive thoughts are known as wise and righteous. Those who adopt negative thoughts are unwise and unrighteous (adharmi). The ways of the world and the spiritual path are different. Always have faith. With faith, problems may not resolved as such, but we develop the understanding so that they don't affect us. Ultimately, it is unwavering faith that gives one stability of mind. Bhagatji said: "One who sees virtues in others, progresses."

ME: How can we develop the qualities of a sādhu while living in this world?

KESHAV: By following the commands of the Satpurush, one can imbibe such qualities. One who introspects can make a discretion between what is the truth and what is not. Yogi Bapa said that there are three types of discretion: to see one's own faults and only see the virtues in others; to believe whatever the Guru says to be the highest truth; and to detach from negative thought patterns and adopt positive ones. To see the flaws and faults of others is itself the very form of negativity. Ego, jealousy and hypocrisy should be found in oneself, not in others. If you see flaws in others, those flaws come into you. You shouldn't see the flaws in others. Don't take everything to heart either.

ME: Can you elaborate on the mind, and how we can develop positive thoughts?

KESHAV: The Upanishads state: 'man eva manushyanām kāranam bandha-mokshayoh, bandhaya visayasango muktyai nirvisayam manah' (the attitude of the human mind is the cause of bondage and it is also the cause of liberation. The mind absorbed in sense objects is the cause of bondage, and the mind detached from the sense objects is the cause of liberation).[2] William James said: "Human beings can alter their lives by altering their attitudes of the mind." You just need to continue to do what you are doing – only differently. Your attitude is the product of your thoughts, and if you change the way you think, you can change the attitudes that you have. There are so many things we can't choose in life but we say we're in a 'free' world? The only thing we can choose is our attitude.

First, empty your mind of negative emotions. Shri Krishna says to Arjun: "Get rid of the cowardice in your heart!"[3] Likewise, we must get rid of the cowardice in our minds. Shri Krishna says: "While contemplating on the objects of the senses, one develops attachment to them. Attachment leads to desire, and from desire arises anger. Anger leads to clouding of judgement, which results in bewilderment of memory. When memory is bewildered, the intellect gets destroyed; and when the intellect is destroyed, one is ruined."[4] When we don't allow for gone-off food to stay in the fridge, why do we let long-term resentment or hatred stay within our minds? Hatred destroys the hater more than the hated. Negative emotions will consume you so much that you won't be able to break free. So, empty your mind.

----

[2] Amritabindu Upanishad 2
[3] Bhagavad Gita 2.3
[4] Bhagavad Gita 2.62–63

Second, fill your mind. Fill them with positive emotions. Your happiness depends not on how many people love you, but on how many people you can love. Celebrities know that the world love them, but why are they miserable? Because of this! They have not learnt to properly love another. The Vedas say: "Oh Lord! Let *me* see everyone as a friend."[5] If you have this outlook, nothing will harm you. Change the way you talk to people. Change the way you talk to yourself. Be the first to change, and then the world around you will change. The only way to get rid of negative emotions is to fill them with positive ones – it's about balance. You cannot get rid of darkness without sparking the light. Start being positive and the negativity will leave by itself. Spark your own light.

Beyond positivity and negativity, there is a third attitude – a spiritual attitude – a selfless mindset. Empty your mind. Fill it. Fulfil it [with spirituality]. This takes you beyond the positive and negative. If you are not spiritually fulfilled, your attitude will change according to your self-interest. Pramukh Swami said: "Prayers save us from misery. Prayer saves one from becoming arrogant."

Look at Shri Rama's coronation! Everyone was preparing, and he was given the news that he had to leave. Now, think about the material versus spiritual approach. Rama and Sita could've easily fought for their rights. They could have confronted or attacked, but this would have been material. Instead, they chose the spiritual approach. Rama accepted his duty. He respected his forefathers. He absorbed the situation and so, he

---

[5] Yajur Veda 36.18

was finally able to overcome everything. We don't know anything that happened in Ayodhya during those fourteen years, but we know what happened in the forest. Why? Because everyone followed Rama. Everyone *still* follows Rama.

When Gandhinagar Akshardham was attacked, what mindset and attitude did Pramukh Swami instruct the swamis to maintain? He said: "Put ice on your head. Blame no one. Don't be negative. Don't think of vengeance or revenge. Make sure there is not a single sign of a bullet or stain. Forgive, forget and move ahead. Our only responsibility is to make sure peace is maintained." What an outlook! You cannot change everything in the world, but you can change the way you look at it. Positivity and peace *always* begins with you.

ME: Divyabhāv – seeing everyone as divine – why is it difficult to maintain this outlook?

KESHAV: Divyabhāv lessens because of our base instincts. We perceive ourselves to be this body, and so, we see faults not only in others, but also in the Satpurush. This destroys our divyabhāv. Only when we eradicate our own faults will we be able to maintain divyabhāv towards others. Whatever is worthwhile in life is in satsang. It seems paradoxical that when we are on the spiritual path that we struggle to maintain divyabhāv. It is only when one earns the grace of the Guru, that the illusion of being one with the body dispels, and only then can one maintain divyabhāv in all things.

In the end, remember one thing. Maharaj said: "Everything and everyone is divine. Whoever understands this principle, thinks about it, and practices it becomes joyous and wins over the world. Day or night, their experiences of bliss never cease to exist."

ME: Kothari Swami and other senior swamis display great composure and patience. Were they born with these qualities or did they develop them?

KESHAV: They were born with them.

ME: How do we imbibe such composure and patience then?

KESHAV: We can imbibe them, but there will always be traces of our old habits.

ME: Then if such impulsiveness is 'inherited', then are we to blame?

KESHAV: Once you realise your base natures, and if you still continue to maintain them, then of course it is your fault! The roots may remain, but if you can suppress them, then you are not at fault. Your capacity to suppress your base nature depends on how much of the Satpurush's teachings you have imbibed in your life and how often you introspect. You may make a mistake but if you remember that 'God and Guru will not be pleased; this does not benefit me', then you will be able to restrain yourself. It is *only* through the Satpurush that such thoughts are inspired.

ज्ञानम्

Samjan

[sum-jun]

spiritual understanding

Powerful kings, emperors, leaders, and the wealthy face misery by fighting and quarrelling over wealth and land. However, those who develop true wisdom experience lasting joy. This wisdom is that of ātmā and Paramātmā. These were the words echoed by Pramukh Swami Maharaj a couple of decades back in a public discourse in India. In reality, it is only through spiritual understanding that we can remain stable in the fierce tides of the ocean of this world and existence. But how do we distinguish the truth from the ignorance? How do we develop lasting spiritual understanding?

ME: What form of samjan (spiritual understanding) should we constantly maintain?

KESHAV: Gunatitanand Swami, explaining [Vachanamrut] Gadhada I-27 said: "Even if someone were to throw dust on me, or were to humiliate me in any way, or were to seat me on a donkey after cutting off my nose and ears; or even if someone were to honour me by seating me on an elephant, all these situations will be equal for me."

Equanimity amidst any situation is the epitome of samjan. Bhagatji said: "Keep equanimity whether our throat is cut or whether we are venerated. Never be sarcastic towards anyone. Tolerate whatever one says and never think badly of another." One will be able to recognise the gunas[1] if one keeps awareness. If a person can recognise

---

[1] the modes of nature, of which there are three: sattva, rajas and tamas

which guna is prevalent internally, one will refrain from indulging in actions related to it and one can maintain awareness. One can achieve equanimity in this way and can also achieve the gunātit state through the association of the Satpurush. When the Satpurush bestows grace upon such a person, he makes one similar to himself.

ME: How should we react to praises and insults?

KESHAV: Yogiji Maharaj used to say that we should remain stable-minded amidst praises or insults. Everyone chases praise. It's all about the status game in the modern world. It's all about protecting the ego. Tolerate as much as needed, especially on the spiritual path.

Steven Covey's eighth habit is: 'Don't expect others to change. Change yourself and others will follow you'. This same habit is written in the Swamini Vato[2]! Gunatitanand Swami says: "Just as we want to make others understand us, if we understand them first, then nothing more remains to be done." We must change ourselves. This will give us control. Otherwise we will continue to wallow in self-pity all our life. Don't blame your own mind either. Maharaj says that the mind is inanimate and simply a tool. It is *always* within our control. Our mind and senses are insentient. It is we who think good thoughts and we who think bad thoughts too.

---

[2] the talks of Gunatitanand Swami, the spiritual successor of Bhagwan Shri Swaminarayan; a commentary on the Vachanamrut

ME: Why do we get happy when we're praised, but not when we're insulted?

KESHAV: We suffer more from constantly ruminating on what others have said or done to us, rather than from any actual incident. Eleanor Roosevelt said: "No one can hurt you without your consent." This is true. We amplify our issues. Alexander didn't remain patient, introspect, or, take a step back, and so he ended up killing his closest friend!

It's all about practice. Just as you fall whilst learning to cycle, you may fall here too, but you will learn. On the spiritual path, this understanding is of utmost importance. Even ātmāvichār (contemplation of the soul) is difficult here, but the main focus should be pleasing God and Guru.

Tolerance is the strongest of virtues. Yogi Bapa said: "By forgiving one experiences a fountain of joy, and the great becomes pleased from within." Was he talking rubbish? Of course not! He lived this at each and every moment of his life! You see, when you attempt to change what is not in your control, you become unhappy.

ME: Maybe tolerating is easier for sādhus (ordained monks). They have the mindset and detachment, we don't...

KESHAV: Sādhutā (saintliness) is not the clothes you wear, it's an attitude. Ninety percent of saintliness lies in tolerating. We don't like tolerating because we feel we need to get revenge at people – tit for tat. For this, we often even resort to sarcasm, which is worse than a sharp sword. Even if you have the capacity to answer back, you shouldn't. You should *always* tolerate. Yogi Bapa never read any psychology or self-help book, nor did he study this field, but what he said is confirmed by today's psychological world. He was one of the most resilient individuals! Yogi Bapa said: "If someone talks to us with sarcasm, do not talk sarcastically back. Tolerating is the same as forgiveness. This way one feels continuous peace within one's heart."

Robert Muller said: "To forgive is the highest, most beautiful form of love. In return, you will receive untold peace and happiness." William Thackeray writes: "To endure is greater than to dare; to tire out hostile fortune; to be daunted by no difficulty; to keep heart when all have lost it; to go through intrigue spotless; and to forgo even ambition when the end is gained – who can say this is not greatness?"

We need to make sure we don't make a mountain out of a molehill when someone says something to us. Without tolerating, one's mind will never remain stable. The more intolerant you are, the more unstable your mind will become. When Arjun was asked to shoot an apple, he was asked what he could see. He said: "All I see is Duryodhan!" See how much he was affected by his intolerance and need for revenge? Maharaj says in [Vachanamrut] Sarangpur 2: "Do not harm another life." This is not just to be done through our actions, but through our thoughts and words too.

Tolerance protects the heart. There is a link between tolerance [in the form of resilience] and happiness. Tolerance is an inner virtue, it is not seen, it is experienced within one's heart. The more one tolerates, the greater he is. Think about what happened to Draupadi! Even Muktanand Swami… he was very spiritually very powerful, yet he contracted tuberculosis. Despite this, he remained joyful. His spiritual strength never wavered in the slightest. He had full conviction in the manifest before his eyes being the all-doer.

Sahanshakti is tolerating power. But the best use of power is its non-use. Has Pramukh Swami ever used his power? Sometimes we feel why is it us that must tolerate even if we're in the right? But Maharaj gives the answer to this. He says that one who tolerates despite not being at fault is truly great. One who cannot tolerate remains stuck in this world. You see, we are in the illusion that we are already liberated, but who knows? The feeling of being liberated is *experienced*. The highest dharma is to tolerate. God believes one who tolerates to be of a heightened spiritual state.

If you have patience, you will be able to tolerate. Patience and spiritual understanding. Buddha said that patience is the best form of prayer. Maharaj said that all spiritual understanding lies solely in tolerance. The crown of all of Yogi Bapa's teachings is tolerance. Seeing divinity, not speaking bad of others, etc., all of this helps the virtue of tolerance flourish.

ME: What about when we face struggles in life?

KESHAV: The problem is that we think *we* shouldn't have to go through struggles in life. But Maharaj says no. The order of sansār is such that hardships will naturally come. Maharaj gave a vivid explanation of this truth to Muktanand Swami and Gunatitanand Swami, who then told Jaga Bhakta. He explained that even the great avatars of God struggled, but this was to set an example for us.

He explained how Shri Krishna was born in a jail. Devaki witnessed the murder of seven of her newborns. Imagine this situation today! Then Krishna had to be moved from Mathura to Gokul. Within a short while, Putna came to try and kill him. Then others also came to disturb or harm him. At the age of eleven, in Mathura, he fought with Kansa. He then went to Sandipani's āshram (monastery) to study. He then came back.

Gunatitanand Swami explained that in the life of Shri Krishna, one of the greatest tragedies was the fact that all of his marriages were made through battles. It is said that he had 16,108 wives. It is said that he had ten sons and one daughter with each wife! Then came the Pandava and Kaurava fight. The war occurred. He came back to Dwarka, the Yadava dynasty drank together, fought each other, and eventually took one another's life. Sons and fathers killed each other! Krishna fought his own brother, Balarama. In front of his own eyes, Krishna witnessed his entire family being killed. In the end, he was shot by an arrow, and he left this world too. This is the reality of life.

Look at the life of Shri Rama too! Without any fault of his own, he had to go into the forest for 14 years! Sitaji herself was never at fault, but even she too had to suffer on numerous occasions. Look at the life of Maharaj and the Gurus. Misery, struggle and hardship is natural. But the fundamental solution is to engage in satsang and develop samjan. Read [Vachanamrut Gadhada] II-60. Maharaj says: "By becoming depressed, crying, etc, one becomes more unhappy. That isn't the solution."

ME: Then what is the solution?

KESHAV: Without spiritual understanding, there is no solution. There is no problem in this world that cannot be overcome with spiritual understanding. All problems are of the body and mind alone, never of the soul. If you believe yourself to be the ātmā – to be Akshar – what problems even remain? Maharaj also says that one should constantly contemplate on one's own death and temporary nature. Look towards one's expectations – how are they hindering you? It is all about samjan. Pramukh Swami said that the wise discipline themselves, the unwise discipline others.

Everyone gets worried in life, it's natural. The main thing to remember is that we must *never* lose faith in God. He is the all-doer – whatever he does is always for the best. He takes birth on Earth for the very purpose of redeeming jivas and giving them permanent bliss. God tests our faith on numerous occasions. He tests and puts us through challenges only so that we can become pure – spiritually more than anything.

Charcoal turns to diamond when it is put under stress. Even we (pointing towards himself), as sādhus, go through trials, but one must always maintain faith in God. Patience and courage is necessary in life.

God controls everything – the good and the bad. Have complete faith in him. He is the source of all happiness. Maintain such understanding. Adverse circumstances are our testing ground. We trust people in this world so easily, believing that they will do good for us. Why don't we trust God? Through faith, one experiences peace. Yogi Bapa lived for God. That was his lifeline. He believed everything to be God's wish.

Joy or misery – destiny is governed by God. He is the one giving us joy. He is the one giving us misery. With this belief, trust God. Be decisive, don't sway. Joy and pain are a part of life. Maharaj said: "Despite me being physically present, joy and misery will remain." God only gives us hardships for our benefit. Whether we realise this or not.

The Pandavas had Shri Krishna by their side, yet they still had to go to the forest. Shri Rama was God himself, but even he had to endure life in the forest. Everything was set on the evening of Shri Rama's coronation. All arrangements had been made. On the eve of the coronation, Manthra turned the tables! This happened to God himself! But God is omniscient, independent and flawless. He sets an example for us. God suffers to ease our pain. Life is replete with joy and pain. Our Gurus didn't have to endure pain, but they suffered to give us strength. Their suffering teaches us not to be afraid – to never despair. Consolidate your faith. Remember that without God's grace *nothing* is possible. No matter how much we endeavour, we cannot achieve success. Human effort and God's grace, both are needed in life.

ME: Stability of mind – regardless of the situation – is the key?

KESHAV: Muktanand Swami has written: "Whatever joy and misery one experiences in life, one must keep patience and courage." Maharaj says that when we face such cycles of happiness and misery – we should remain calm and patient – we should not become upset or frustrated. One should offer prayers and continue to persevere. Sometimes, it may be the cause of fate.

Look at the earth. Sometimes it is soft, sometimes it is hard; sometimes there are pebbles, and at other times it is as smooth as sand. The layers of the earth keep changing. In the same way, we will undergo change and such phases and variations in our life too. We will experience 'ups and downs' too. Always persevere. And even if while persevering in your endeavours, the situation still doesn't change, understand that it is God's wish and whatever he does is for our betterment alone.

Faith in God can solve all problems. Man believes: "I am doing everything. I will make the world, family and society happy." But this is nothing but arrogance, and where ego operates, there is always downfall. God is the sole doer. It is he who does everything.

God is the doer in this world, in our life and in our country. When one has faith in God's doership, he can then realise his ātmā, attain success in life, be happy and peaceful in all ways.

With such courage and patience, strengthen the force of bhakti and satsang in your life. You should remain equipoised in all circumstances. The body is an ocean of miseries. Circumstances will befall all. Regardless of who it is, everyone has experienced difficulties and will continue to do so. But those who have kept faith in God have progressed and remained at peace. Never lose hope. This is the fruit of spiritual endeavour – the progress of the soul – that is the greatest thing.

ME: Many talk about the 'inner-eye' opening. If this is true, when does it open?

KESHAV: The inner eyes are said to open when you have assimilated spiritual knowledge. The Satpurush, who is brahmaswarup (the very form of Brahma), imparts this knowledge. Hanumanji had such eyes, so he was able to recognise Rama. Tulsidas could not. But when Hanumanji explained and Tulsidas understood, he recognised Rama. When the Satpurush gives knowledge, the inner eye opens. When knowledge is perfected, dharma is perfected. When dharma is perfected, no bad thoughts will remain in the mind. That is why you should not be [purely] affectionate, meditative or enthusiastic – particularly on the spiritual path but instead, one should cultivate knowledge.

ME: How do you remain happy and at peace?

KESHAV: Spiritual understanding (samjan) is the root answer. One will remain happy to the extent one exercises vivek (discretion) in one's life. Everything else is hollow and temporary. Everything that happens is due to the grace of God and Guru. I truly feel that I don't do anything, and so I feel peace, peace and peace! Maharaj says: "One attains happiness based upon one's understanding." This is the understanding you need to develop.

Those who have spiritual understanding are immersed in spiritual joy. Regardless of their situation, they live joyously all of the time. True wealth is spiritual wealth. Many experience this form of pure bliss here itself. Despite the lack of material wealth, their inner bliss transcends everything. One is fully content through the association of God and Guru. It is like the happiness of the entire universe. With such an understanding, one experiences bliss 24 hours a day. We, too, have to attain that bliss through wisdom. One who does that will face no problems. When you have attained satsang and the Satpurush, what more is left to be attained? Nothing! It does not matter if we attain anything else or not. In the end, it is all short-lived. Living happily with such an understanding, one is always able to live in peace. Never be in doubt of such things. God and Guru should be the prime focus, and this way, one is blessed with eternal happiness and peace.

The nature of the world and being immersed in it, is like sitting on a camel. It is a bumpy ride. We have to adjust to the bumps to avoid pain. If we don't adjust, we get hurt. Similarly, in life, we have to learn to face up and adjust to the bumps. Liberation lies in believing God to be the all-doer. Everything happens solely due to his wish. "If we doubt, we suffer downfall."[3] Remain content under any circumstances. We came here empty-handed and we will leave in the same way. Cultivate such spiritual understanding. Keep a singular thought that God is the all-doer and that happiness and peace is only achieved through him.

ME: You've previously spoken about the five types of powers in human beings. Could you explain this?

KESHAV: Of course. There are five types of power in human beings: body power, mental power, brain power, ātmā (soul) power, and Paramātmā (God) power. These are inherent in all of us, but how we choose to use them is up to us. We fall ill or we're healthy. The immune system plays a key role in this. This is body power. You can have as much body power as possible, but without mental power, you will spiral.

Alexander conquered the world, but he failed to conquer himself. He died at the age of 33 from a disease, not even from old age! He killed his friend and army chief, Cleitus the Black. Then he felt great remorse. He conquered everyone but not himself. To

_____

[3] Bhagavad Gita 4.40

conquer oneself is mental power. Brain power is quite obvious, it's important to function. The Vedic tradition focuses on mental power. Purify the mind. Improve the mind. Everything begins in the mind. The mind plays about most when it comes to our ego. People have committed suicide because of their ego or status!

The deepest craving of human beings is to be appreciated. It isn't wrong as such. It's nice to be important, but it's more important to be nice. To be important is modern. To be nice in spiritual. Spirituality is not physical, it's all mental. Sitting in a meditative posture is not mental, it's physical. Meditation is in the mind – it's mental.

ME: What is the need to be honest in life?

KEṢHAV: (laughing gently) This is actually a modern-day question. There was never a question of honesty before. Society today – individualistic thinking – has brought about this question. When we strive for our own self-interest, this question arises. The fruits of honesty are not seen immediately. They are seen in the future. It becomes a central, foundational quality of one's life.

Remember, character is power. Look at Gandhi! Churchill was fearful of Gandhi, and even Hitler was scared of Churchill! How can we forget that it was because of Churchill that the Second World War was won! But it was Gandhi's character that gave him value. Through honesty, all other qualities slowly enter one's life. If you are honest, you will remain content. If you are dishonest, you will always feel uneasy. On the outside, your life may look amazing... but inside... (shakes head).

ME: How do we remain calm and undisturbed?

KESHAV: Gunatitanand Swami says: "There are two ways to remain calm and not get disturbed. One is to engage in devotion and, secondly, think of God as the all-doer. In doing so, accept whatever comes, by way of happiness or pain." We embrace happiness easily. But, when inflicted with pain, we tend to shy away and we can't tolerate it. Never evade whatever little pain we have to face, instead, tolerate it.

Kuntaji asked Shri Krishna to bestow *more* misery upon them! Why? So in that way, they can remember God more. God has kept us in a simple state and that is best. We are guests here... for 50, 60 or 70 years. Our unhappiness stems from a wrong sense of 'I' and 'mine'. King Janak was above this sense of 'I' and 'mine'. He believed himself to be the ātmā, to be Akshar, or, Brahma. He lives with this sense of detachment. He cultivated true knowledge.

Misery is inevitable. Suffering is a choice. Our scriptures have echoed, from the outset, that there are three types of pain: disease (ādhyatma), misery inflicted by other living beings (ādi-daivi), and natural disasters (ādi-bhautik). We will always face these three types of misery. But during them, we should remember God, take refuge in him, and engage in bhakti. This gives us comfort. When we don't get upset and remain calm, our mind becomes stable. No thoughts can disturb us. Turn towards bhakti for strength. You will experience joy.

ME: Ultimately, it comes down to detaching from outcomes, acceptance, and believing God to be the all-doer?

KESHAV: (nodding his head) Yes. Gunatitanand Swami said that the soul is *never* satisfied. As soon as God relieves one misery, the soul craves for relief from the next. He explains that fate is determined by God's wish. Obey his commands, persevere and work hard. Do not keep asking of God all the time either. Do not crave for too many material things. Accept what comes. Let go of what isn't.

You are bound to face difficulties in life. No two days are the same though. Difficulties are bound to arise due to the nature of existence. Joys and sorrows both will come. It doesn't matter who you are. But those who do not have spiritual understanding, suffer. When faced with difficulties, they become disheartened and feel unrest throughout life. But one who has faith in God, cultivates a strong spiritual understanding. Such a person remains at peace.

Tolerate. Willingly accept and face all circumstances. This is what we learn from the life of God himself. The greater the faith we have in God, the happier we will become. Only have one thought. If one continues with patience, courage and strength, gradually matters will improve in life. One with spiritual strength overcomes all difficulties with ease. Spiritual strength is the most powerful – the strength of God – the strength of dharma. Faith is imperative. Faith is the mother of all. Without faith, one loses heart. One becomes confused and loses direction in life. One with faith will never be troubled.

ME: If God is the all-doer, can't we assume that when someone commits a wrongful deed, it is in fact God doing it?

KESHAV: (shaking his head) No. God only inspires us to do good. When someone does wrong, he does so because of his own nature and desires. God has given us the common sense to distinguish between right and wrong. Despite this, because of our own weaknesses, we knowingly do the wrong things. Then it becomes a habit. In the end, it is only we who suffer the consequences.

ME: Doesn't God protect us?

KESHAV: He does, but when? Only if we make a mistake without realising it. Committing a wrongful act on purpose is not a mistake, it is a sin. For that he doesn't protect.

ME: What about all of the natural calamities and disasters that occur in the world? Is God responsible for that too?

KESHAV: That is the power of kāl (death). Remember this. Only God – not you, not me – only God knows what is best for humankind. Man begets the fruits of his actions. You can't blame God. Everything happens at its appropriate time (creation-destruction). The world is forever changing. These are the facts of life which we have to accept. So rather than being upset or sad because of such events, you should pray instead. Otherwise such thoughts leave us bitter and resentful.

ME: What causes one's faith to waver and disbelief to arise?

KESHAV: Unfulfilled desires are what degenerate faith to become disbelief.

ME: How do we develop perfect conviction and faith?

KESHAV: By developing intense affection and oneness with the Guru, we automatically reach such a state. Apart from that, there is no need for any other endeavour. If we can realise that only *he* can lead us to liberation, then *he* is the all-doer who inspires us in all our activities. *He* is the giver of moksha. This way, we will automatically develop a strong bond with him. Our 'selfishness' for the Guru helps too. Just as we love our family – because we know that only they will provide us food, clothing and shelter, if we realise that only the Satpurush will give us moksha, then because of this form of 'selfishness', we build a deep attachment towards him.

As long as you consider yourself to be the body, there will always be a distance between you and the Satpurush. But if you can believe him to be your true form, then instantly, you become one with him. However, it takes time to remove the age-old perception of being the body. In the meantime, keep persevering in satsang.

Maharaj says: "Not to waver in times of difficulty is a greater test than the fire tests. Only a wise individual who knows himself as the ātmā passes such tests; others are unable to pass. Such an individual becomes happier the more he faces difficulties. He understands that nothing is unknown to the indweller. Also, he realises that the ātmā has no misery; for misery is related only to the body and mind. He has firmly established the principle that the body is never going to be happy."

ME: Life seems full of disappointments…

KESHAV: Hardships and difficulties are encountered according to fate. We have to accept that. But the more punya (spiritual fruits) one earns, the more one's sins are dissolved. We can also lessen our mental burden by seeking refuge in God and Guru.

One should keep total faith in them in all activities, but one should never live according to superstitions. Remain strong. Only when gold is heated in a furnace does its colour develop. It is only when God tests a devotee that his love for God recognised.

When we carry out any task, our intentions determine the type of fruits we earn. A man may give charity to help the poor, he may visit the temple regularly, but if his objective is to please God in the hope of being rewarded with more wealth, then that is what he will receive. If one does something with a desire to attain specific ends, he will receive just those fruits. But if he desires nothing for himself – except for the sole intention of pleasing God – then he will not have to take another birth, for he receives the ultimate fruit of all endeavour: moksha.

Life exists and with it, comes responsibility. It isn't easy to live in today's social climate considering the state of the world. However, we should keep God at the forefront of all our activities and learn to be content with whatever we get in life. We shouldn't become depressed. Believe that everything is God's wish and keep going.

Samjan is the root answer. All questions are solved through samjan. Doing things out of understanding will sustain your spirituality, whereas other [worldly] things will come and go, stay or disappear. Through samjan, one can experience all types of happiness. We don't need to 'let go' of anything as such in life, we only need to develop samjan.

King Janak remained detached through samjan. He was the guru of even the son of Veda Vyas! Nothing outside harms us, what is within us is what harms us. Live in the world, but remain detached from the world. It all comes down to faith. God and Guru have no selfish motives. God may put difficulties into our lives so that we don't become attached and glued to this world. The ocean may be violent on top, but in the depths, there is tranquility and peace. Develop such understanding and you will remain detached.

ME: It seems like such a difficult task… to cultivate all this spiritual understanding.

KESHAV: One with understanding never feels that worldly misery is real misery. The greater one's status, the more forgiving one must be. Knowledge of any type without God is the form of ignorance. One's wisdom is reflected in one's actions. Whatever understanding there is in satsang all resides in tolerance. The more one tolerates, the greater one becomes. Without difficulties, there is no happiness. As long as one has desires for anything but God, one experiences difficulties. Without tolerating, bliss is not attained.

When difficulties arise, if patience is maintained, then peace remains. There is no greater understanding than to have patience. The greater the patience, the more courageous one is. If patience is lost, everything is lost. The more forgiving one is, the happier one becomes. Judgement is required in forgiving. Miseries never come to one who has both vivek (discretion) and forgiveness. Nishkulanand Swami writes: "Nothing is greater than patience." We should cultivate such knowledge and understanding. There is no need to give up anything, we just need to foster wisdom like this.

Jaga Swami said: "First become a human. Imbibe truthfulness, non-violence and the vow of non-lust firmly. Then you are human. After that worry about becoming ekāntik[4]. How does one remain constantly good? Vachanamrut Loya 17. To shun one's body, to associate with one's ātmā, to detach from the five senses and engage in bhakti. One who constantly strives to progress in these four areas remains good." Yogi Bapa said: "Master [Vachanamrut Gadhada] II-11 and develop understanding like Sitaji.

Faith in God and Guru is the most important quality one can imbibe. It is of utmost importance. If one has faith, they are already on the path of moksha. Moksha is liberation from all vices and base natures.

---

[4] the highest spiritual state in which one offers bhakti (devotion), along with dharma, jnān (knowledge) and vairāgya (non-attachment)

Sankhya

[sank-yuh]

impermanence

A man, tired of his monotonous life, visited a psychiatric doctor. He was advised that he needed amusement in his life, and for this he was told to visit the circus. He told the doctor that he already went to the circus three times a day. The doctor said: "No, but in the circus there is a clown by the name of Grimaldi. Go to see his show, and I guarantee you'll be rolling on the floor in laughter!" The man replied: "Doctor, I am in his show three time a day, but I still want to die!" The doctor was confused: "How is that possible?" The man sighed and said: "Sir, I am Grimaldi."

Whether the story of Joseph Grimaldi, the son of a deranged Italian immigrant (also one of England's most celebrated clowns) is true or not, his situation is reflective of the human dilemma. People see us as being happy externally, but only we know what is going on within our minds.

Hitler came into power in 1933, after Germany lost World War One. He created an army and won over Europe in a couple of years. He came into power and got rid of Jews. He planned to kill every Jew, and he *did* kill 6 million. But he also ended up killing himself with the same gun that he was going to use to kill the last Jew with. Death is certain.

Julius Caesar ruled over one of the largest Roman empires, but he had a fear that he would die alone in darkness. To rid of this fear, he stayed amidst people. When it got dark, he would hide under his blanket and sleep in fear. Caesar died amongst people, killed in the day, by his own friend. Death is certain.

Napoleon remained one the most powerful leaders for twenty years. He had a fear of water, believing that it would be the cause of his death. He died with water in all four directions around him. Death is certain.

Genghis Khan had a fear that his killer would be a youth, and so, he kept sixty attractive women around him, as to divert the attention of any youth that approached him. He even put in his will that wherever he goes, anyone that crosses his path should be killed. Genghis died with sixty attractive women still following him. Death is certain.

The Russian dictator, Stalin, killed 60 million Russians. He had a fear that his death would be caused through poison. To keep this fear at bay, he kept fourteen doctors close to him. If medicine didn't work whenever he fell ill, he would have the doctor in charge assassinated. Through this alone, a mass exodus of doctors occurred. His fear even caused him not to eat warm food towards the end of his life; he ate it after 12 hours, once people had taken bites of the food, so that he could check if they died. Stalin died from food poisoning. Death is certain.

In the same way, Gandhi didn't know it was his last prayer. Kennedy didn't know that 'no, you certainly can't', were going to be his last words before he was shot. Death has been created in a mysterious way. Everything around us may seem stable, but life itself is unstable. To develop true stability of mind, we need sānkhya vichār (contemplation of the impermanent nature of all that exists).

KESHAV: Everyone has expectations for happiness. People want lots of wealth, a big house, a luxurious car, holidays, loving children, and a beautiful partner. We also want no problems! Maharaj says: "Even if you have all this, if you don't have sānkhya vichār, you will not be happy." To develop this thought process means to be constantly aware of the temporary nature of all that exists.

What do people in this world do? From dust to grains and from grains to dust! If one understands just this, then one is able to detach from everything. One who is detached doesn't harbour anger, ego, attachment to the body, and other such vices. Like Yogi Bapa used to say: "Whatever, however, whenever and wherever, adjust." Detachment itself is adjustment and tolerance. Contemplate on the temporary nature of existence daily. This world, realm, and everything within its existence is perishable.

ME: If we develop such a thought process, won't that make us indifferent and irresponsible towards ourselves, our loved ones, and also to the world at large?

KESHAV: There is no happiness without sānkhya. Even Shri Krishna says: "All created beings are unmanifested before birth, manifest in life, and again unmanifest at death. So why grieve Arjun?"[1] This is similar to how water passes through three stages. First there is water, then there is ice, and again, it becomes water. Before, we were unmanifest; now, we are manifest; then soon, we will be unmanifest again. This

---

[1] Bhagavad Gta 2.28

understanding is to be understood and applied to oneself, not towards others. Maharaj himself, contemplating on the nature of death, says: "I think that I will die right here, right now."[2] Such understanding is difficult to confront, but it is needed.

The countdown for our death begins from the moment we are born. Deep down we know this, yet we continue to run after fleeting pleasures. Why? If a rich man or a pauper meet the same fate? Tolstoy said: "How much does a man need?" The very definition of sānkhya yoga is to believe everything to be perishable. There are four bondages of humans on earth: places, people, possessions, and vocation. Maharaj concludes: "After studying *all* the scriptures, I have concluded that everything stemming from māyā is perishable and insignificant."

ME: How and why do we need to develop such a thought process?

KESHAV: Gunatitanand Swami said that we should think about the perishable nature of the world. Yogi Bapa said that we should learn to tolerate, adapt and live under any circumstances – however favourable or unfavourable. Cultivate samjan [a positive spiritual understanding].

We may have a nice house, valuable assets, a successful business and many such comforts. Yet, we still expect and desire more and more. We want our name to be in

---

[2] Vachanamrut Gadhada III-30

the ranks of the highest earners. We lose ourselves in such desires. And if this is not achieved, we become disheartened. We should not harbour such desires. With God's wish, we should certainly work hard – we need to sustain ourselves within society – but at the same time we should remain satisfied with whatever we get. One who is content with 'what is' remains happy. If we keep craving for more and more, our desires will only get fuelled further. It is purely due to our expectations that we become unhappy. There is no other reason. Expectations and attachments. The world is perishable; one day it will be destroyed. Remain constantly aware of this. If we continually do so, we won't experience misery when we face pain.

ME: What will become of us if we remain attached?

KESHAV: Why are you taking others' problems onto your own head? First sort out your own! Besides, what could possibly happen to us? Keep your focus on ātmā and Paramātmā. Maharaj says that everyone is attached to the obstacles of wealth and women, and that there are no worse faults than lust and greed. The attachment or detachment towards the world is recognised by the dreams one has. That is what Maharaj says. No matter how much fame you have in this world, after death, nobody remembers. It is all short-lived.

Yogi Bapa used to say that up to our neck, we are filled with the 'world' and so we don't understand and believe what the Satpurush tells us. If one develops true wisdom, one is never infatuated by worldly desires – infatuation dissipates. There are four barriers to overcome: realise Purushottam, realise the Satpurush, realise the ātmā as being distinct from the body, and detach from even the highest pleasures. If you do this, you will experience nothing but bliss!

ME: Is pain relieved through such a thought process?

KESHAV: Yes. As well as bhakti. Learn to forget the past. This itself is sānkhya vichār. It teaches us: 'janmyā tyāthi jarur jānvu, marvānu chhe māthe ji…' (know that from birth, death is hovering above our heads). It is a fact that we will all die at some point in the future, so why grieve about it? Even when God incarnated on this earth, he had to leave and return to his abode.

This form of humility takes one closer to God. Forget the sense of 'I' before God. That is what we have to do. 'Vayam amrutasya putraha' (we are all children of God). By being his, we attain happiness and peace. Just as you live here as a guest, you should live in this world as a guest too.

ME: To attain liberation, is sānkhya most important?

KESHAV: You need both sānkhya and yoga. Most tend to focus on yoga, but don't have clarity of the impermanent nature of everything else around them. You need love for

God and Guru, but you also need to understand the impermanence of everything. You need bhakti, but not just any bhakti, you need ekāntiki bhakti. Whenever the mind goes astray, pull it back. Then don't allow it to go again. To control the mind, one requires sānkhya. It's very important! If Mirabai and Buddha left everything, there must be something to this!

ME: What is māyā?

KESHAV: Ignorance. Anything that obstructs one from knowing ātmā and Paramātmā is māyā. It is like a web that even the most powerful become entangled within. Māyā is anything that is tempting, baiting and decoying. On the surface there is brilliance, but inside there is darkness. A person who has knowledge of ātmā and Paramātmā is never trapped by māyā.

ME: What is knowledge?

KESHAV: To believe one's ātmā to be above the three bodies, three states and three gunas. Bhagatji said: "This body is like a pit hole of hell: it is perishable and insignificant. On the other hand, the ātmā is the very form of happiness and is incredibly powerful. It is divine, full of bliss, and it is eternal. It cannot be cut or pierced. It is ageless and immortal. Believing it to be distinct like this, one should develop oneness with Sachchidānand (i.e. Aksharbrahman; the Satpurush)."

ME: How is that oneness developed?

KESHAV: Bhagatji explains that too: "Firstly, all the universes should be destroyed mentally through total detachment. Then, having resolved that the following four – one's ātmā, the divine abode, the liberated souls and God – are left and nothing else, one should behold God's form within one's ātmā. Thirdly, one should attach oneself to God, in the same way as a partridge is lost in the moon, or a lustful person in women, or a greedy person in wealth. Through this thought process, one should shun any worldly objects that create an obstacle. By practising this, one should become brahmarup and achieve the state of continual oneness with Purushottam. After that, there is nothing more left to achieve. There is no escape without doing this. Through the ekāntik, one becomes ekāntik. Apart from this, liberation cannot be attained by even a million other means."

Bhagatji was the personified form of sānkhya. He said: "Introspect and think to yourselves how we put full endeavour into the place from where will leave at any moment! This is the greatest ignorance of the jiva. A person's desires for the sense objects are, in fact, characteristics of an unholy person. One cannot be happy whilst one still has a weakness for women or wealth. When one overcomes this weakness, discards body-consciousness and discards base instincts, only then will one attain happiness and peace."

ME: Death is certain for everyone. So why are people still afraid of death?

KESHAV: Because there is ignorance. Because of ego. When you realise that the soul has a different existence from that of the body, all fear is lost. Maharaj himself says that one should do everything in life, but only with the understanding that one day we will suddenly have to leave it all. If actions are done in this manner, detachment develops slowly.

The youth feel death doesn't touch them, and the elderly feel that death is around the corner. The paradox is that the one who feels that death is far, is closer to it. The one who feels death is close, is further from it. The laws of nature always prevail, death is certain for all.

Shri Krishna says: "Death is certain for one who is born."[3] The more science tries to prolong life, the more they discover how fragile and temporary human life really is. We sometimes forget we will die! We don't like talking about death, we do everything to prolong life. Everything in life is a probability other than death.

Live in this world and do everything, but remember God and live according to his commands. Then there will be no problems at all. Otherwise, if you go to any person of this world, you will only get material happiness for the body.

---

[3] Bhagavad Gita 2.27

Shri Krishna said: "Oh Arjun! In your mind you believe that all these are my relatives and friends, but this is mrutyulok[4]. Everyone has to leave from here! Leave this belief that you have in your mind and take my refuge…" We endeavour to find out what life is for our entire life, but the moment we understand what death is, the meaning of life will become clear before our eyes. The awareness of death gives us the ability to do good unto others.

---

[4] literally, 'the realm of death'; the only realm in this cosmos where human birth and liberation is possible

एकता

Samp

[sump]

unity

Harmony begins at home. When harmony enters your home, success, wealth, happiness, and health all follow. Harmony is the source of happiness; it sustains it and helps us share it with others. Happiness follows harmony. Although happiness has to be inclusive, we all want to remain exclusive. Happiness has to be sustainable, but we all want to sustain ourselves at the cost of others.

Combined research from the London School of Economics and the Paris School of Economics interviewed 200,000 people. They wanted to find out what it was that makes individuals happy or miserable. The results were astonishing. They found that education plays a role of less than four percent role in making someone happy or sad. Money plays less than three percent of a role. But it is social relationships that plays a role of more than 80 percent towards a person's happiness! Research even shows that the happiness chemicals – endorphins, oxytocin and dopamine – can all be boosted through maintaining and developing positive relationships with others.

Sigmund Freud said: "Civilisation is a process whose purpose is to combine human individuals, after that families, and then races, people and nations into one great unity – the unity of mankind." How far civilisation has served its responsibility is questionable. They do say the world has become smaller, but unfortunately husbands and wives, parents and children, brothers and sisters, teachers and students, friends and loved ones are moving further and further apart. Today's sorry state is ironically portrayed by the American poet and playwright, T.S. Eliot: "[TV permits] millions of people to listen to the same joke at the same time, and yet they remain lonesome." Man has probed deeper and deeper into the atom, in a quest to comprehend life, but he cannot understand his own brother. He has learned to see millions of light years into unknown space, yet fails to peer into the heart of the neighbour.

As one race, we sail the same oceans, soar into the same skies, scale the same mountains and stride the same earth. Nature does not believe in segregation; the sun shines on all – no questions asked. Shakespeare writes in *Merchant of Venice*: "Does not every man have eyes? Does not each human have organs, dimensions, senses, affections, passions? Is his hunger not satisfied with the same food, his thirst quenched by the same water? Is he not hurt with the same weapons, subject to the same diseases, healed by the same means; warm, cold and wet by the same seasons as any other man? If you prick him, does he not bleed? If you tickle him, does he not laugh? If you hurt him does he not cry? If you poison him, does he not die?" It is indeed true that underneath different shades of 'armour', everyone's blood is red. Then why so much disunity and disconnect?

Pramukh Swami taught: "The world is our home, humanity is our nationality, mankind our countrymen, truth is our anthem, tolerance our flag, love is our language, kindness our religion, and the Great God is our Father." The Upanishads say that the whole of creation is filled with the presence of God. The Yajur Veda also says that the whole world is one nest.

ME: Why should I maintain samp if no one else does?

KESHAV: Samp always begins with you. By expressing samp only when others do so, then, there will be no end to conflict. Such an [attitude] results in ruin. So, [to create or maintain samp] we should think about what we can do, what type of thoughts we should have, and the words we should say. Do not look at what others are doing or not doing. We should express samp from outside.

ME: How do we resolve issues within the family and experience peace?

KESHAV: By trying to understand one another. Especially between couples, a husband should think: "How can I become a good husband?" and a wife should think: "How can I become a good wife?" Subsequently, there will be minimal conflicts and even court cases between them! The fifth habit of the seven habits is itself: first seek to understand and then to be understood. This is of paramount importance.

ME: When someone makes a mistake, should we just tell them as it is?

KESHAV: When someone errs tell them, but do so with politeness (vivek), humility (namratā), by believing them to be yours (potānā mānine), and for the good of their soul (jivnu rudu thāi).

ME: But isn't it said that it is impossible to understand another human being, so how do we even attempt to?

KESHAV: To understand another often seems as difficult as climbing the Himalayas! This is because of the ego – because of 'I' and 'mine'. We feel that when we have to understand another, it's a punishment for us. But, in fact, it is fundamental to our inner peace. It is a technique. Yogi Bapa, the one who has understood others the most, said: "No matter how another is, to still see them as divine is the essence of all spirituality."

Many books have been written on understanding others, but Yogi Bapa and Pramukh Swami have lived this! You need to first understand yourself – why do you think the way that you do – only then can you seen to understand others. Sometimes, we don't think and we just spurt out words. We don't think about how it may affect another person. We must take a step back and think before we speak out. Like Bhagatji said: "Examine your words before speaking."

We eat, but we don't know how to eat properly. We sit, but we don't know how to sit properly. Similarly, we all speak, but we don't speak properly. Yogi Bapa said: "Use words like milk. Don't talk too much much. Always keep sugar in one's words. Our words should be such that people love us. This way we feel peace within." So, think twice before you speak. Four things can never be returned: a shot arrow, a lost opportunity, a passed life, and spoken word. First listen, then think, and only then speak.

We are all playing ego games [shakes head]. Try to make Pramukh Swami's life your ideal. He has lived by his words. He hasn't simply preached; he has *lived*. He has given the solutions to all of life's issues through his own life and experiences. If you want me to be truthful then listen: people do the opposite of what's right. But just remember that without *his* association, we are nothing. View everything through the eyes of gun-grahan (thinking and looking positively).

ME: What are the benefits of performing gun-grahan?

KESHAV: There are many benefits! Maharaj himself has said: "Let it be that one does not perform my [personal] service, but he speaks and thinks of the positive qualities of another, that I consider him as having performed my personal service." So, by looking towards the mahimā (inherent greatness) of other individuals, you can experience inner peace. Pramukh Swami said that bhakti itself is to see everything and everyone as divine. The fruit of all endeavours is to see everything as divine. We struggle to understand the greatness of things as they are. One benefits to the extent one wishes good for others.

ME: How do you perform gun-grahan?

KESHAV: Simply do not look at [others'] negative traits. Everything else that remains [to think about] is gun-grahan.

ME: Is there a technique to doing this?

KESHAV: One should have a firm resolve that they want to look at the positive qualities of others. Adopt no other mindset. Only then is it possible. You should see the positive in *everyone* in this world. If there is something positive we can learn from someone, then we should do so, regardless of their background or beliefs.

ME: Don't you get bored of only seeing the positives in others?

KESHAV: No, how can I get bored? It is a positive action; it is beneficial! Maharaj becomes pleased! So it should be done repeatedly. Gun-grahan is sevā. To focus and think about the negative qualities of another is a very negative thing to do. You ruin your life and inner peace, and also that of others' too. It is very detrimental, but we fail to realise this.

ME: What benefits do *you* experience from this?

KESHAV: I experience joy... Immense joy! Performing gun-grahan is enjoyable. I am also immensely pleased with one who performs gun-grahan without telling another.

ME: What if in doing so, we go off-track and see another's faults? What should we do?

KESHAV: A cat holds its kittens with its mouth, and with that same mouth, it catches a mouse and kills it. The same example applies here – these thoughts come naturally. One does not harm those for whom one has affection. However, we should not forcefully rebuke another and say things such as: "Why are you doing this?" or: "Why aren't you doing this?" One should maintain discipline and think: "They will improve… if not today, then tomorrow."

Thoughts of others' flaws happen [naturally] but that happens because one wants to see others improve. But instead, we should pray for them and think about what we can do to help them. Maharaj asks: "For one who does not appreciate the greatness of others, how long will one's own greatness remain?" For the significant self-interest of the individual, people malign each other. There is no greater disaster than the mind remaining impure, and so we must stop finding flaws in others.

ME: But if someone has many obvious flaws, and I see it before my eyes, how do I see the positive in such circumstances?

KESHAV: Through tolerance and acceptance. One day they will improve. It isn't your responsibility to change another person; you can only change yourself. But always keep the right intent and pray [for them]. Remember that no matter who it is, anyone can take things wrongly. So never be under any form of delusion that you won't offend anyone. Think twice before you speak or react. Maharaj goes as far as saying: "If allegations happen to be true, one should constructively advise the person in private, but in no way should one be publicly humiliated."[1]

ME: Should I perform gun-grahan proactively, or only when negative traits are seen in others?

KESHAV: When negative traits are seen, that is when one should *definitely* perform gun-grahan, and in general, one should always try to see the positive. There is only benefit in doing so. If one sees another's faults, they regress a lot. The damage is only done to oneself. With this, one needs humility. Humility is like packaging. All other qualities reside within humility. Without it, there is no unity.

ME: What stops us from seeing the positive in others?

KESHAV: One's own base natures. We *need* to develop tolerance. We *need* to keep patient. Maharaj has said that to see one's own faults and the virtues in others is paramount. Pramukh Swami said that finding faults in others is like licking excreta. Yogi Bapa said that through the service of others, we find the peace of God. Seeing the good in others *is* the service of others. We *have* to tolerate. Rama went to Kaikeyi's home first upon returning to Ayodhya and hugged her. Learn to forgive too. Pramukh Swami's example at Gandhinagar Akshardham is the epitome of forgiveness. It is *we*

---

[1] Vachanamrut Gadhada I-72

who should be tolerating others, instead of others tolerating us. Even Gunatitanand Swami said that to stay together and understand each others' glory is the 'fifth difficulty', but it can surely be overcome.

ME: How important is love towards all?

KESHAV: Without love, there is no scope for understanding. The world is sustained on love. Take out love and everyone in this world would become demonic. The philosophy of terrorism is this: hate and kill. The philosophy *we* must go by is: peace and love. Take love away and we are just like machines and robots. Look at some parts of modern society today and you will see this. We all need to adopt the virtue of suhradpanu (cordiality).

Unity is the power of God. Where there is unity, there is success, prosperity and divinity. Where there is no unity, there is never peace. In unity lies material wealth, spiritual achievements and godliness. There, a divine ambience forever prevails. That is why to see a human as a human, is humane; but to see God in a human, is divine.

ME: How should we develop true relationships?

KESHAV: The crux of every relationship is trust. You are the common factor in every relationship, and so, you must adjust yourself. Manage things within you and take charge of your relationships. The Upanishads say: 'yasmin vijnāte sarvam evam vijnātam bhavati' (knowledge received through the transcendental is so perfect that by that knowledge one becomes acquainted with all different manifestations of the supreme being).[2]

Maharaj says: "He who sees everything around him, but fails to see what is within him, is the greatest of fools." Pramukh Swami said that so long as you don't realise yourself, you will identify with the 'I' and you will not be at peace. So, know yourself. We are taught that in life that our importance is based on how many people love us, but the quality of your life depends on how many people you love. And ultimately, it only the love of God and Guru that is selfless.

ME: Controlling our speech is important, right?

KESHAV: Indeed. Always be more of a listener than a talker. Silence is golden, so talk less. Shastriji Maharaj said: "Use your words like ghee[3]." Yogi Bapa said: "Use your words like milk." So think before you speak. Don't keep talking. You can never take back the spoken word. Draupadi spurted, "A blind man's offspring are bound to be blind!" Look what that led to! It makes you think doesn't it, what really caused the Mahabharat?

––––––––––––––––––––

[2] Mundaka Upanishad 1.3
[3] clarified butter – a rich ingredient in India at the time

Yogi Bapa said: "Talk that which is the truth. Talk that which is beneficial. Talk that which is love." Ninety percent of arguments stem from one's own words. Our intentions are reflected through our words. Giving praise is not hypocrisy. This is what some may think, but it is a sign of respect. You should *always* give respect to one and all through your words, regardless of how another person is. Look at the positive side.

ME: How do we remain stable, and also maintain unity and harmony when we're not even in the wrong?

KESHAV: That will automatically happen if you bear such words in mind. If you can tolerate someone insulting or ridiculing you, then you won't have any problems. By constantly tolerating, you will feel that honour and insult are one and same. But if you get angry and confront another, then it's game over! Just as we feel good when someone praises us, we should feel just the same when we are insulted. Stability is the ability to still have love for the aggressor.

ME: But if someone insults us, should we stand up to them, otherwise we look weak?

KESHAV: The perpetrator is the weak one. We should simply tolerate. The thought that 'I am so popular and I've been made to look weak' only comes to mind because we are body-conscious. Realise that you are the ātmā and these superficial thoughts won't affect you. How does tolerating make us weak? Be optimistic. Everything else is irrelevant. Tolerating is the path of a sādhu. Believe that the greater a person's tolerance, the greater the person's intrinsic power. The foundations of one who can tolerate are immoveable. Maharaj says: "To forgive is not just child's play, but it is like an open war!"

ME: The generation gap often creates huge differences in opinions in beliefs. This means there is constant friction between the young and old. How can this be resolved?

KESHAV: It is natural that elders tend to be orthodox whereas youngsters are full of new ideas. However, to say that any one group is the cause of friction is wrong. Youth are not ready to accept the advice of the elders and the elders are not ready to adapt to the views of the youngsters. Basically, both groups should try to understand each other. If they can learn to compromise, there will be no problems. Always make an effort to understand and tolerate one another.

ME: What about other the ego of others? People want praise and acknowledgement. How do we cope?

KESHAV: Know that this is to do with the base natures. All we can do is tolerate. To maintain balance and peace, someone needs to adjust. Become the bigger person and tolerate. Whilst maintaining fraternity, unity and divinity, never speak bad of anyone. Even if it is the truth, do not speak that which will harm another. Even if one causes us harm, never retaliate and cause harm. Even for the sake of your own esteem, never harm another. Do not see the flaws in another. Tolerate. Where there is unity, there is peace. God resides where there is unity, and victory prevails where there is unity. However, whatever, whenever, wherever – learn to adjust. Learn to tolerate. Learn to see the positive side. There is no happiness like that. One who tolerates, progresses.

Bhagatji Maharaj said: "Those who see virtues in others, progress. Never speak negatively, always see the positive." If someone insults you or harms you, and you are still able to see them as divine, at that point you know that you have conquered your ego. As long as your minds are not one, there is no unity. We must maintain unity, regardless of whether another does or not.

Pramukh Swami's words sum this up entirely: "Unity in diversity is the lesson of life. Flourishing together is the secret to peace. Just as the unity of believers makes faith strong and stable, unity of faiths will make our future strong and stable. Religion is that which spreads love for one another. Let every religion exist and flourish. At this hour in human history, we religious leaders should not a dream of only one religion in the world, but dream of a world where all religions are one – united. We must remind ourselves that every civilisation, culture and religion born on this earth is like a gold mine, rich with values, wisdom and vision."

"Children are the wealth of our society and nation. Like the scriptures say: 'āno bhadrāhā kratavo yantu vishvataha' (let noble thoughts come to us from every side). Yogiji Maharaj often said: "Think not that mine is the best, but that whatever is best is mine." The Upanishads say: "In everyone and everything, there is the divine presence of God." The Vedas say: "We are all the children of God." Bhagwan Swaminarayan says: "We are all ātmās – pure spiritual entities, unattached to and unbound by caste, country, race and religion." The Mahabharat says: "Behold all living beings as oneself." There is nothing more important than engaging in a dialogue with oneself. In the good of others, abides our own. In the progress of others, rests our own. In the joy of others, lies or own."

Satsang

[sut-sung]

spiritual association

F. W. Robertson said: "It is not the number of books you read, nor the variety of sermons which you hear, nor the amount of religious conversation in which you mix, but it is the frequency and earnestness with which you meditate on these things till the truth which may be in them becomes your own and part of your own being that ensures your spiritual growth."

ME: How important is spirituality in life?

KESHAV: All humans seek peace. True progress itself is to be peaceful at all times. Maharaj says: "This jiva has drank as much milk from the mother as there are drops of water in the ocean."[1] What does that mean? We've been here so many times, and we are back here now! Buddha said something similar when he said that man has cried as many tears as there are drops of water in the ocean.

We sit in a car, train, bus, or plane, and we love looking out of the window. We love to watch TV and movies and look 'out there'. Man loves looking outside but seldom does he look within. For true progress, one needs to look within. This is achieved through satsang. Pramukh Swami said: "The heart of education is the education of the heart." That is satsang. You can change your hairstyle, dress style, anything, but unless you

---

[1] Vachanamrut Gadhada III-39

change your mindset and lifestyle, no real change will be made. Satsang and ekāntik dharma[2] is the only means to pleasing God and Guru.

Society may seem to progress with technological growth, but without spirituality, we cannot progress in the truest sense. Technology is like a stone in comparison to spirituality, which is like gold. Man may have made immense technological progress, but without spiritual wisdom, one will never achieve peace in life. Only through satsang can one discriminate between the eternal and ephemeral. Satsang is what enables one to enjoy the bliss of one's ātmā. For physical illnesses one needs medicines, however, for spiritual troubles what does one do? For that one needs jñān (spiritual knowledge).

ME: What is satsang?

KESHAV: To keep the company of those who are true and good. With the company of good people one is inspired by wholesome thoughts and is able to maintain one's integrity. Keep away from the company of one who is critical of others, because he will spoil your buddhi (intellect). Like a rotten potato by its association, keep away from such people. The purpose of a mango tree is to produce mangoes. The purpose of a banana tree is to give bananas. What is the fruit of satsang? It is to be redeemed of dehabhimān (attachment and ego for one's body).

---

[2] a term for the combination of dharma, jñān, vairāgya, and bhakti

Satsang is that in which no attachment to the mind and senses remain. In fact, the sole purpose of the senses and the mind is to practice satsang. There is no joy greater than that of engaging in satsang. Without the refuge of satsang, one cannot live in this world and yet remain detached. Maharaj says that without satsang, life is worthless. As long as one craves for happiness in things other than satsang, understand that one has not understood the importance of the human body. True Satsang is that in which, once attained, one feels no form of deficiency. It is about experience. It is the association of the truth.

ME: What is the goal of all spiritual endeavour?

KESHAV: To develop unflinching faith in God and Guru. How is this done? Maharaj says in [Vachanamrut] Vartal 11: "Intense love for the Satpurush is the *only* means to realising..." Only satpurush – not God *and* Guru – love for the Satpurush is the *only* means to realising the ātmā and Paramātmā.

Always prioritise satsang. We've taken countless births. We've become kings and even devas (deities) like Indra and Brahma in the past! We become unhappy when we continuously wallow in self-pity. Everything you hear here isn't mere speculation or imagination – it is facts. True peace can only be found within satsang. There is no need to seek proof, validation or guidance from the world for peace – you have it right here.

The 'ABC' of satsang is to realise one's ātmā to be distinct from the body. Only then will all of one's spiritual endeavours be accomplished. As long as one's body and ātmā are entwined with one another, no efforts [for moksha] will bear fruit. In satsang, there is [inner] light for one who perceives virtues and there is darkness for one who perceives faults in others. One who does not waver even amidst misery can be said to have developed true satsang.

ME: Does spirituality help with life's problems?

KESHAV: There are so many questions that bother everyone. Questions regarding both our physical and mental health. Questions to do with family issues, social issues... There's so much. None of our solutions work against the avalanche of life's issues. But there is one thought that does work, and that is in understanding that God is the all-doer. His will prevails, good or bad. This is the solution to all our problems. It is the ultimate principle. The answers we seek are to be found here. If we really understand and apply this principle, the answers we seek are to be found here. Our problems will seem like a pile of dirt before a vast mountain range like the Himalayas.

There is a story from the life of Dr. A. P. J. Abdul Kalam. He appeared for an aircraft pilot interview in Dehradun. Only eight candidates were to be selected. He came ninth. Having just missed out, he felt deeply dejected. Then, opposite from where he was, he saw the monastery of Shivanand Swami. He went inside and the swami said to him:

"Why are you upset, my son? You did not become a pilot due to God's wish, so why worry? Understand it to be God's will and always remain content." And after this life-changing incident, Kalam himself said: "I never became an aircraft pilot, but today, I have made a spacecraft that flies much higher and faster." That day, the swami told him: "Whatever happens is by God's wish." This is conviction. No matter what happens to you – good or bad – accept it as God's will and be happy. Remain spiritually strong and never fall back. God's wish means that whatever he does will turn out to be good [for us]. If we apply this formula to solve all our problems, we will be happy. This is a fundamental principle that we must learn.

ME: Is moksha attained through satsang?

KESHAV: Of course. Gunatitanand Swami did say that liberation cannot be attained without knowledge. That knowledge is only acquired through satsang. It is the knowledge of ātmā and Paramātmā. Kings like Janak and Ambrish lived within society, but lived equipoised in knowledge. They engaged in worldly affairs, but remained untouched. Despite the obstacles they faced, they never lost faith in God.

True happiness comes from the removal of ignorance and replacing it with knowledge. Ignorance refers to the I-ness and my-ness that we possess, This is an illusion. Once we die, what is ours? What we think is mine or me is nothing. We become unhappy solely due to our arrogance. Our ego brings us unhappiness.

ME: Why do we need to follow dharma?

KESHAV: It is only when dharma is first firmly entrenched in one's life that any other spiritual realisation can be had. If we possess land that is fertile and covered with wild growing bushes and trees, and on that land we throw the finest of seeds, would crops grow? Of course not! First the land must be cleared of all trees and bushes. Similarly, as long as our minds remain dirty and impure, we will not be able to serve God. This is why we have been commanded to have pure āchār-vichār (conduct and thoughts).

As Maharaj says: "Only where there is dharma is there bhakti (devotion) and jnān (spiritual knowledge). Where there is jnān, there is vairāgya (detachment). And where there are all four of these, God is manifest and moksha is attained. This is the divine essence of the Vedas, Smrutis and Puranas. All benefits reside in dharma. As long as dharma is sustained, one is superior to even the great kings."

ME: What is jnān?

KESHAV: To always remember that whatever God and Guru do is only for the best. That is jnān. Then whether they call us or not, we will be forever cheerful. Look at Tyagvallabh Swami and Kothari Swami.[3] They have never withered in their love and devotion. To always see God and Guru as divine – that is jnān.

---

[3] senior swamis in the BAPS fellowship

ME: What is bhakti?

KESHAV: There are many types of bhakti. Firstly, bhakti can simply be listening to spiritual discourses, having darshan (to see God or Guru), or even staying in the company of God and having a friendly conversation; even making him laugh is a form of bhakti. Then another type of bhakti is dāsbhāv, where one becomes God's servant and carries out his commands without hesitating. For example, when Shri Rama instructed Hanumanji to go to Lanka, he set off alone without thinking twice.

The greatest form of bhakti, however, is ātmānivedanam – which means to surrender one's self entirely at the lotus feet of God. After that, we consider everything that is ours to be his, and offer them to him before using them ourselves. Yogi Bapa also used to speak about annuvrutti bhakti, where one who lives according to the inner, unspoken wishes of God and Guru. So, for example, when they tell you to study or to even do mālā, that is bhakti.

ME: Is performing bhakti for the Guru the same as performing it for God?

KESHAV: (nods head) Yes. [Vachanamrut] Vartal 5.

ME: I feel as though I am not making as much progress spiritually as I should be... How do I make up for this?

KESHAV: To begin with, continue to read scriptures and continue to follow the path of satsang. The path you have found is the right one, but now, continue to walk according to the direction of the Guru. Look to him for inspiration in all your endeavours. By his grace, everything will work out.

ME: On the spiritual path there are many paradoxes which remain debatable.

KESHAV: Religion is a subject of faith. Logical explanation will never suffice. Experience will always override all logic.

ME: Doesn't satsang also refer to keeping good company? Maharaj tells us that we should shun the company of those who are like ourselves. What does that mean?

KESHAV: There, Maharaj is referring to one who has bad habits similar to ourselves. If we enjoy good food and drinks, and we keep company of someone who always enjoys them, then our habits will only increase. We should sit with the pure – who follow dharma, jnān, vairāgya and bhakti – even if they are the same age. Never sit with pessimists either, for not only are they disillusioned, but they also make others disillusioned too. By associating with the pure, one becomes pure.

ME: Pramukh Swami Maharaj and you are an ocean of virtues. If I want to imbibe your qualities into my life, what do I have to do?

KESHAV: Read [Vachanamrut] Gadhada I-67. Always bear it in mind.

ME: Could you talk about the three gunas (modes of nature) and how one can know which one they are under the influence of?

KESHAV: The mode of tamas is seen in those who show anger in every little thing. They don't listen to anyone, and they believe that they are always right. In rajas, one has thoughts of indulging in pleasures such as good food, sights, etc. In sattva, one has noble thoughts, wants to perform austerities, service, etc. Even within sattva, there is rajas and tamas. Likewise, for the other two... they are all intertwined. But that's a topic for another time. It requires deep contemplation and understanding. But know that whatever you do as per the wishes of God and Guru, whilst performing satsang, becomes *nir*gun. This is above all three gunas – it is behaving as the ātmā – as gunātit, or, akshar.

ME: Aren't we always under the influence of the three gunas though?

KESHAV: They will always be there, but we can be immune to their influence by observing the commands of the Satpurush at any time, any place, anywhere. By following his commands we become purified – we realise that we are the ātmā and not the body. But beware never to find faults in others.

Sadhana

[saa-duh-naa]

spiritual endeavors

Life is all about moving from one endeavour to the next. From a young age, individuals strive for success and knowledge through endeavours. But often, we forget the most important striving, that is, to know the soul. All efforts that one does by thought, word and deed to achieve the final goal of their life, is called sādhanā (disciplined and dedicated spiritual endeavour).

ME: What should our sādhanā be?

KESHAV: The essence of all philosophy – anywhere in the world, throughout history – is to know thyself. It doesn't matter if you know everything that might be going on in the world, if you don't know what goes on inside you, it is all futile. Unless you know yourself, life is meaningless.

We are drowned in information, but not even one drop is going into us! It's about how much you do with what you know. What do we need to know? Our attainment. Everything else is mere information. Kabir says: "The happiness found in the Sādhu cannot even be found in any amount of riches." There's no need to close your eyes and try to search for something within. You will only see darkness. See *he* that is in front of you. That itself is samādhi. If you believe Pramukh Swami to be your ātmā, that is equal to knowing yourself.

Wherever one seeks prestige, position, or status, there is only unease and misery. Become the servant of the servant. Look at Pramukh Swami. Despite all the praises and positions, he saw himself as nothing. He said: 'Nārandā chhej kyā!' (Nārandā[1] doesn't even exist). All sādhanā lies in rājipo (pleasing God and Guru). That is all of satsang. That is all sādhanā.

ME: It seems like one needs bravery to have this level of endeavour.

KESHAV: Indeed. Be so brave that you scare your senses and mind. You don't need to win over other people's minds, win over their hearts. But win over your own mind. Don't major in minor things. We are Brahma, we just fail to realise it. You *are* the ātmā. The root of ignorance is the false identification with the body. Read 'The Art of Ruling' Vachanamrut. Believe yourself to be Pramukh Swami Maharaj.

ME: How do I conquer my mind? How does the antahkarana work?

KESHAV: The chitta is a camera – it captures everything without discretion. It is then that the buddhi (intellect) steps in. It decides what to pick out and what to leave out from everything captured. In this way, it maintains a form of discretion based on what it likes. The manas (mind) then constantly contemplates on those objects of desire. The ahamkār (I-maker) unites with the object of desire and makes it a part of one's

---

[1] the name of HH Pramukh Swami Maharaj when he first got initiated as a swami

presumed identity. That is how the antahkarana works. That is how we remain body-conscious. King Janak contemplated on this and was able to maintain discretion. Maharaj said: "I like a yogi who never trusts his own mind." We can *never* trust the mind. We need to stay within dharma. Shravan (listening), manan (thinking), nidhidhyāsan (constant contemplation), sākshātkār (spiritual realisation) – these are the steps needed to conquer the mind.

ME: What is antardrashti (introspection)?

KESHAV: Maharaj has said: "To look towards the murti of God within one's heart or, the one manifest before the eyes, is introspection." True introspection is to do introspection of even introspection. To look towards God and Guru means to understand their wishes and command. Introspection is nothing more than to compare one's life with the wishes of God and Guru, and see how much they align.

Our mind listens, through the ears. Our mind sees, via the eyes. Everything is to do with the mind, and that is why to look towards the murti in one's heart is most important. Maharaj says in [Vachanamrut Gadhada] II-8: "Any action performed for God [i.e. bhakti] is itself introspection. Looking towards the life of the gurus is introspection. We learn from their lives. Anything done for the body is bāhya-drashti (outerspection). That which is done for the soul is antar-drashti (introspection). The technique is one and same. If you have a firm resolve, every step of your life is a form of introspection.

Remember, all change is internal. It doesn't matter if we get to the moon or to Mars, the most significant changes we need to make will always remain internal.

ME: How did you become a sādhu? We've heard that you had difficulties in becoming one, how did you overcome them?

KESHAV: That is a personal matter (chuckling). My mother didn't want me to become a sādhu, everyone else was okay. But to seek the permission of my mother was very important. Once, when my mother and I were alone at home, I hung from a well and she came running out telling me to get out. I said: "Only if you allow me to become a sādhu!" She was left with no other choice but to give me permission (laughing gently).

ME: Didn't Yogiji Maharaj also test you?

KESHAV: In my youth, Yogi Bapa used to show me lots of care and affection, but when I became a pārshad (a renunciate in white clothes), I thought I'd get more care and affection, but the opposite happened! Yogi Bapa didn't even look at me or ask me anything, let alone speak to me... for three months! I thought to myself: "What has happened?"

During my time as a pārshad, I felt tested a lot. I was once woken up at 3am on a day of a fast and was told: "I know I have tested you a lot, but I have given you the fruits of millions of years of penance in that!" From then on, I received immense care and affection from Yogi Bapa. To live according to the wish of the Guru is fulfilment. Sādhanā is to do what the Satpurush says. I never got upset, because I always felt that whatever Yogi Bapa did was always for my best.

ME: How did you develop this level of understanding?

KESHAV: Faith and love.

ME: How do I develop such understanding?

KESHAV: Faith and love. The Satpurush loves *you* immensely. All you need is dradh priti (intense love) towards him.

ME: How do *you* manage to remain so fresh amidst so much activity?

KESHAV: By not feeling that I am doing it or that I have accomplished anything (laughing gently). I believe God to be the cause of everything. He is the all-doer. With this belief, one does not feel burdened. I am not the doer. God is the doer. With such faith, we should all serve until there is life in this body. By doing so, you will experience bliss 24 hours a day. Forgetting body-consciousness, perform all activities whilst remaining focused on God and Guru.

We only feel strain if we believe *we* are working hard. Our efforts are not for our body or our personal happiness; they are for God and Yogi Bapa and Pramukh Swami. If you accept that we have been given this body to serve in this manner, you feel no strain. Don't keep the load on your own head; hand it over to God. If we perform sevā sincerely, we will experience eternal joy.

ME: Are mobile phones useful or destructive?

KESHAV: Pramukh Swami had an allergy towards mobile phones! As useful as they may be, more often than not, they are misused – that is a guarantee. Today, we live in a society where we *need* mobile phones, so vivek (discretion) is key, otherwise one becomes addicted to these gimmicks. Access to anything in the entire world is now in the palm of your hand, before it wasn't like this!

People might feel this is backwards and overly-traditional, but it's not about *who* is right, it is about *what* is right. We must get over the individualistic mindset and get over ourselves too! When I was travelling from Entebbe to Gulu with Yogi Bapa, we boarded a plane. We had nine passengers, but the pilot said he would only fly with five. Yogi Bapa told him that we were all thin and didn't weigh much, so why not? The pilot said: "Five is five! I don't want to die!" Then, some of the passengers came in a car behind and arrived after five or six hours.

What happened there? There must be a reason right? It is probably something technical that is beyond our comprehension and understanding. Likewise, some commands may be beyond our comprehension and understanding. We rely on faith. You cannot apply your buddhi (intellect) in obeying āgnā (spiritual commands). That will only plunge you into a pit. But, apply your heart, which means following commands with bhakti. Self-restraint has the power to reconstruct a crumbling world, and it begins with the individual.

ME: Why must we have a sādhanā?

KESHAV: God gives peace and happiness to all. We can tap into that through rituals and sādhanā. I personally know that these practices have given peace to many. The body will perish, so we must worship God. Yogi Bapa used to say: "The body is like a disposable plate. It's of no use other than to worship God. That is eternal, everything else is transient. There is no alternative to bhakti." Just as gold can be purified by heating it, similarly, through rituals and austerities, the jiva is purified.

ME: What is the best spiritual sādhanā?

KESHAV: To cultivate divyabhāv (divine feelings) towards all and to maintain nirdoshbuddhi (pure and faultless perception) towards all.

ME: What is meditation?

KESHAV: Thinking of God's glory. Contemplating on God's divine glory, his works and reflecting that God who is everywhere, is also within me. That is meditation. It takes constant practice; it cannot be achieved overnight. It develops slowly. Because we are so engrossed in social affairs, we experience difficulty in applying our mind. But with practice and association of God and Guru, our focus becomes sharpened.

ME: What is dhyān?

KESHAV: It's similar. It is to contemplate on the greatness of God. To think about his importance and his creation. To realise that the same God, who is inherent and present in all things, is also within us. Remember God with every breath we take.

ME: What is samādhi?

KESHAV: (listing the steps of ashtāng yoga) That is more difficult to achieve. But through spiritual practice one reaches jnān-samādhi (realisation through knowledge). Then nothing is left in your mind except God. One acquires a higher level of understanding. Then comes brahma-jnān, which is to realise Brahma as a pure and realised being. To recognise his form (swarup) and to accept that God himself resides within him (sākshāt birājmān).

ME: How can I perform ashtāng yoga?

KESHAV: (after observing me and looking me up and down) Instead of aspiring to perform that, reach above its steps and aim for the very top. Now is the time to take a less demanding approach. With ashtāng yoga, there is always the risk of failing halfway. All you have to do here is to learn to love God, do bhakti, dhyān, sevā and bhajan. We've found the purest Sādhu. Attach yourself to him. Follow his commands and relish the bliss of satsang.

ME: What is satsang?

KESHAV: Affinity with God. He is the eternal truth – along with scriptures, dharma and the Satpurush. If one can find such a Satpurush, one automatically attains the other three. The Satpurush instills God within, nurtures love for the scriptures, teaching one the true interpretations of the holy texts. He inspires one to live according to dharma. In essence, satsang is the Satpurush.

ME: How will I know I have attained liberation here itself... the end of sādhanā?

KESHAV: Sādhanā is lifelong, but you will know when you'e become brahmarūp. How? You will become like Pramukh Swami Maharaj. That is your true form.

ME: When one attains this state, does one see God?

KESHAV: The fulfilment of this journey is when you realise that God is right there before you. But we should not aspire for such things, however, if he [the Guru] decides to show you, then it's fine. One who is attached to the Satpurush is attached to God.

ME: You talk about seeing everyone as divine and as Brahma. How do we do this?

KESHAV: First, realise yourself as Brahma. We've come onto the right path, so we *will* attain realisation. If not today, then tomorrow, but one day for sure. Everyone is inherently divine. If you realise this, you will realise what association means.

Every individual is on their own path, leave it up to God to decide how and when they improve. If we keep this in mind, we won't have any problems. Even if others are bitter or sour, God will tend to them. We only need to be cautious that nothing hinders us on our path. If it really troubles you, tell the appropriate person, but don't become obstinate and go around gossiping or seeking revenge on futile matters. It's not proper that we cause problems for others.

Satpurush

[sut-poo-roosh]

*the Sadhu who has constant rapport with God;
the Gunatit Sadhu or Guru*

Humans, to a greater or lesser extent, are narcissists. We are all in love with ourselves. We overly care and have concerns for our own bodies, and then, for our significant other, children, parents, siblings, and finally our friends. The Guru shines apart here. Like the 18th century British historian and essayist, Thomas Carlyle, rightly said: "The greatness of great men is known by the way they treat little men." Worldly personalities attract limited groups of people, and even then only for a limited period of time. Whereas the divinity of God within the Guru pulls people of all ages and abilities, all beliefs and backgrounds, all tribes and cultures.

The famous English writer, William Somerset Maugham, on meeting the renowned sage, Ramana Maharshi, in India, writes: "It is a mistake to think that those holy men of India lead useless lives. They are a shining light in the darkness. When a man becomes pure and perfect, the influence of his character spreads so that those who seek truth are naturally drawn to him."

In the BAPS tradition, Bhagwan Shri Swaminarayan's divinity continues, through the living, breathing spiritual Guru – to guide, bless and inspire the lives of millions of individuals, and ultimately, lead them to the path of moksha. Speaking about his Guru, Pramukh Swami said: "Even if he's not saying anything, we still experience happiness – because there is sweetness within. There is God within, and we experience that bliss… Through him we are liberated. Through him we attain peace. Through him our base instincts and desires are washed away and cleansed; we attain God's abode."

ME: What is the need for a guru?

KESHAV: Adi Shankaracharya says: "The Vedas with their six limbs and the knowledge of all sciences may be on one's lips; one may possess the poetic gift and may compose fine prose and poetry; yet if one's mind be not centred upon the lotus feet of the Guru, what then, what then, what then?"[1]

The essence of the Shrimad Bhagavata Purana is shared by Kapildev to his mother Devhuti: "If a person maintains profound love towards the Sādhu of God (the Guru) just as resolutely as he maintains profound love towards his own relatives, then the gateway to liberation opens for him."[2] Out of the 18,000 verses of the Bhagavata Purana, the scholars have chosen this verse as the essence. The Mahabharat also says that knowledge is the ship that takes us across the ocean, and the true guru is its sailor.

To defeat māyā without the aid of the Satpurush is impossible. One has to associate with the Satpurush through one's mind (man), action (karma) and speech (vachan). There is no person like Pramukh Swami Maharaj in this entire world. Dr. A. P. J. Abdul Kalam experienced profound peace in the presence of Pramukh Swami. He said: "In Pramukh Swami, I felt and experienced the direct energy of Bhagwan Swaminarayan. He was the perfect embodiment of all virtues." Maharaj says: "Having attained this

---

[1] Guru Ashtakam
[2] Shrimad Bhagavata Purana 3.25.20

human body, one may become even a king, but without the company of the Satpurush, all of it is worthless. Those who associate with the wise Guru, are freed from the net of attachments."

The Guru is our role model. If one maintains love and trust in the Satpurush, everything is understood. To look at the ātmā within is not introspection, but to look at the manifest ātmā (the Guru) 'out there' and introspect on that with wisdom is true introspection. One who has love for the Satpurush has already attained moksha. Through the association of the Satpurush, one's attachment to the body is diminished and humility, along with bhakti, develops. Nobody other than the Satpurush can do what is beneficial for the jiva.

In almost every Vachanamarut, Maharaj talks about the Guru, he just uses different words like 'sant', 'satpurush', or, 'motāpurush'. The Satpurush vaccinates the jiva. It may hurt a little, but one will experience peace and joy within. One will become fearless. The Guru attaches those who come into contact with him to God, who is above him, but he never attaches them with himself. In the Mahabharat, Yudhisthir says to the Yaksha: "Logical reasoning is not without bias (assumptions), Vedic revelations are numerous, not one thesis can be accepted as facts, truly the essence of dharma seems very subtle and secretive. The only recourse is to walk in the footsteps of great men."[3]

---

[3] Yaksha Prashna, Mahabharat

All the ancient scriptures speak of the necessity of the Guru, who is the human form of Brahma. The Upanishads sing: "He who knows Brahma, becomes like Brahma,"[4] and, "Not through much learning is the ātmā (Brahma) reached. Not through the intellect and sacred teaching. He is reached by the chosen of him. To the chosen, the ātmā (Brahma) reveals his glory."[5] Maharaj says: "Whoever believes the great Purush to be absolutely free of flaws becomes totally flawless himself."[6] By knowing him, one goes beyond death; there is no other way by which one can go there, 'tameva viditvāti-mrutyumeti nānyaha panthā vidyate-yanāya'.[7]

Knowledge cannot be attained from books alone. Association with the Satpurush is a must. If by merely reading one could become a doctor, why do children have to go to school? To obtain spiritual knowledge, you *have to* associate with the Guru.

ME: Is the guru God?

KESHAV: According to [Vachanamrut Gadhada] I-27, God constantly resides within the Guru. The Guru is not God, nor does he ever become God, but he is *like* God. God works *through* the Guru. This is the ultimate level of divyabhāv. God always resides in his

---

[4] Mundaka Upanishad 3.2.9
[5] Katha Upanishad 1.8.23
[6] Vachanamrut Gadhada I-73
[7] Svetasvatara Upanishad 3.8

divine abode, but through his divine will he can manifest his form anywhere in the cosmos. The Satpurush is Akshardham. God resides him in entirety. Like Nishkulanand Swami said: "With the self lost in God, God pervades him." The one sitting is Brahma. The one sitting within [the Guru] is Parabrahma.

Shri Krishna states his close bond with the true Sādhu saying: 'sādhavo hradayam mayham, sādhunām tu hradayam tvaham' (The Sādhu is my heart, and I am the heart of the Sādhu). The Guru is the gateway to moksha. He guides, encourages and blesses us to attain moksha. Pramukh Swami said: "God is the Guru of all gurus – Gurunām guruhu."

It is through the life of the Guru that we can understand God. The Shrimad Bhagavata Purana echoes this: "Through the incidents of the Satpurush, one is informed of my valour. The ears and heart hear my discourses, which are comparable to the form of a medicine. By listening to those discourses, ignorance becomes defunct and faith, devotion and love manifest towards God."[8]

ME: Is it extremely difficult to realise the true Guru?

KESHAV: Shri Krishna was on earth for 120 years, but still many did not recognise him! Duryodhan didn't see him as God. Pramukh Swami lived on earth for 95 years, did *we*

---

[8] Shrimad Bhagavata Purana 3.25.25

recognise him? God worked through him. How did someone who barely passed sixth grade achieve so much? The role of the Guru is the bestow moksha, thus allowing us to realise God. The Guru *must* be manifest. That is a must. That is the way to moksha.

ME: What should we do once we have attained the guru?

KESHAV: Yogi Bapa once said: "To contemplate on wherever the Satpurush has sat, slept, eaten, etc., is brahmavidhyā." The greatest of all endeavours is to develop love for the Satpurush. One should not act according to one's wishes in front of the Satpurush; one who is wise, is able to let go of one's negative behaviours. Always see the Satpurush as divine. Think about [Vachanamrut] Vartal 9.

One wants to develop the qualities of the Satpurush, but one does not look within and introspect. According to [Vachanamrut] Vartal 5, if we see the Satpurush as flawless, we become flawless. As we see him, so we become. Yet he always remains unfathomable and above all. Love for the Satpurush itself can be understood as the destruction of desires. Gunatitanand Swami said that one should learn all the attributes of the Sādhu that are written in the 11th chapter of the Shrimad Bhagavata Purana, and in the Kapil Gita, as well as in the story of Bharatji.

To live according to the wish of the Satpurush bestows divine grace. Maharaj says: "Whatever the Satpurush forbids is known as adharma." In this world, everyone's mind has become their guru. To get rid of that, make the Satpurush the true guru. Fight the mind constantly. If we go against the wishes of God and Guru, we experience misery. If we live according to their wishes, then we experience peace, peace and peace. You may do a million things that your mind wants you to do, but to do just one thing according to the wish of the Guru is greater. Do whatever it takes to live according to the wish of the Satpurush. However and whatever must be done to the mind and body. Never doubt the Guru. As long as doubts remain, the light of Brahma is not seen.

ME: Through the Satpurush we attain moksha?

KESHAV: There are three types of karma: sanchit, kriyāman and prārabhda. Who destroys prārabhda karma? The Guru. This is explained in [Vachanamrut Gadhada] I-58. The attainment of God and Guru is itself liberation. God and Guru are the greatest. There are none greater. If one develops such understanding, one experiences peace. Give your mind over to the Guru. How do you know if you've given your mind over? If he says something, you have no doubt in doing what he says. When the Satpurush becomes one's mind, that is true bhakti and seva. Moksha is to associate with, understand, and live according to the Satpurush.

The more you associate with the Guru, the more you benefit. Through the association with the Satpurush one acquires wisdom, and wishes, desires and misery are eliminated. The Satpurush is satsang. Dedicate one's body, mind and wealth to the

Satpurush. To behave as such means to give your life to the Satpurush. Yogi Bapa said: "The scriptures talk about the nine types of bhakti, but to sacrifice oneself entirely for the manifest form is the tenth form of bhakti."

King Rahugan says to Jadbharat in the Shrimad Bhagavata Purana: "A person who engages in profound spiritual association with the divine great Purush cuts delusion with the sword of knowledge, reflects on the divine actions of God, and through bhajans and listening, attains knowledge of his own form and also attains the supreme God. That is, they become engrossed in and merge with God."[9] Maharaj says that serving the Satpurush is itself moksha. There is no other meaning of moksha. Only a few really understand this. Those who do, and serve the Satpurush accordingly, are considered liberated. He even says: "The essence of infinite talks is that one should recognise the Satpurush. When this is done, all spiritual endeavours should be considered complete."

ME: What is faithfulness?

KESHAV: To obey every wish of the Satpurush. When the Guru is pleased, then the desires developing from the five senses dissipate. That which we wish to attain after leaving this world, we have attained right here, right now.

---

[9] Shrimad Bhagavata Purana 5.12.16

ME: What is a pilgrimage?

KESHAV: The Satpurush. Wherever God and Guru have travelled, that place itself is a place of pilgrimage.

ME: What is manifest dharma?

KESHAV: To follow the commands of non-lust, non-greed, non-attachment, etc., according to the wish of the Satpurush is manifest dharma. In short, whatever the Satpurush says is itself dharma.

ME: What is brahmavidhyā?

KESHAV: To recognise the personified Brahma and to develop love for him.

ME: What is meant by Brahmajnān – knowledge of Brahma?

KESHAV: The Satpurush is Brahma. To understand his spiritual glory and perfection is brahmajnān; to believe that God is fully manifest in him is brahmajnān.

ME: Who is the most unfortunate?

KESHAV: One who doesn't recognise the manifest form of God and Guru.

ME: How does one attain the grace of the guru?

KESHAV: By doing as the Satpurush says. By adjusting for him. If he says it's night, it's night. If he say it's day, it's day. That's how. The home of happiness is the Satpurush. This world is temporary, destructive, minute and frivolous.

ME: Can you tell me about Pramukh Swami?

KESHAV: No matter how much you know him, he is beyond and beyond. Pramukh Swami always wanted to help. Whether a person was a Hindu, Christian or Muslim did not concern him. The human condition was the same everywhere. There was ignorance. If ignorance were removed and replaced by God-consciousness there would be supreme joy. Pramukh Swami wanted to teach this truth to everyone.

ME: But Pramukh Swami has gone, now what?

KESHAV: (shaking his head) No. Pramukh Swami Maharaj has not gone. (pointing a finger to his chest) He is right here.

ME: So the Guru is necessary?

KESHAV: (firmly) Absolutely.

ME: Are you saying that without a guru, one cannot attain God?

KESHAV: That's right. Just like when we go to school, we only acquire knowledge by learning from the teachers.

ME: But there are many who educate themselves...

KESHAV: Even they need books don't they! The book becomes their guru.

ME: So then why only follow one guru?

KESHAV: If one approaches many gurus, they will teach him different things. Then what does he accept? So then nothing substantial is achieved.

ME: How does one mentally offer devotion to the Guru? And how does the Guru himself do bhakti?

KESHAV: One sees God and Guru to be totally faultless. No matter how the Guru may behave, he never doubts his actions. Whatever the Guru says, he accepts as the highest truth. With such faith, one attaches himself to his guru and then bhaktyanuvruttya – he observes the inner wishes of his Guru – that is bhakti. The Guru offers similar devotion towards God. He believes God to be the all-doer, free from evil instincts and human weaknesses. He is, in a word – nirdosh (flawless).

The more bhakti one has towards the Guru, the more peace he experiences and the more his soul progresses too. On the spiritual path, a guru is an essential guide. In Indian life, the Guru is the whole and soul – he is everything to the disciple.

The more bhakti the disciple has, the more peace he will experience here and hereafter too. The disciple believes that God himself resides in totality within the Guru. Thus, the Guru is able to bridge the gap between the devotee and God.

ME: How much can one achieve through the grace of the Guru? And if one wishes to earn such grace, what is it that one must do?

KESHAV: The life of Bhagatji Maharaj is the perfect example for every aspirant. No matter what, where, or when his Guru commanded, he obeyed it wholeheartedly, without any question. The fruits of such devotion is the direct realisation and experience of God.

ME: Why is the Satpurush present on earth?

KESHAV: The Satpurush is here to redeem countless souls and he never forgets that. In fact, he is always thinking as to how he can help souls. He may call someone and ignore you, at times he may even scold you, but in his eyes, he sees everyone as equal. Because of our base instincts, we feel, "Why does he talk to that person and not me?" But he has no such discrimination. We must always maintain divyabhāv towards the Satpurush.

ME: What greatness did you see in Yogiji Maharaj?

KESHAV: (after pausing for a few seconds in deep thought and answering slowly) Yogiji Maharaj is a true Sādhu. God resides within him fully. He is the form of God. God resides in every part of his body. He beholds God in his heart. In his abode, God resides as himself, but here, he is one with the Guru.

ME: Does God dwell in the Guru fully or only to a certain extent?

KESHAV: God pervades throughout his whole being.

ME: So then the Guru is the form of God?

KESHAV: When God incarnates in the form of a king, he acts like a king. He rules over his kingdom, attends to the affairs of the state and even wages war. When he incarnates as a Sādhu, he portrays the characteristics of a Sādhu. However, both are forms of God; there is no difference between them. Just as the ātmā resides in the body, in him resides Paramātmā.

Thus, realising the Satpurush to be the form of God, we should offer our devotion and sevā towards him. In effect, we are offering to God. If we realise that the Satpurush is the form of God, then everything else will pale into insignificance. Only God and ourselves will remain.

ME: If God is forever present on earth through the Guru, then why is that the knowledge of God disappears? And how is it that such a lineage of Gurus also stops?

KESHAV: Maharaj tells us that a jiva can never be destroyed. But by being given the form of an immobile object, for example, a mountain or a rock, it is as good as being destroyed. Thus, the jiva cannot attain the knowledge of God.

In the same way, the Satpurush and the knowledge of God are *always* present on Earth, but due to circumstances, sometimes that knowledge cannot be preached openly. Then, even in the presence of the Satpurush, such knowledge disappears. Maybe after two, five, or even ten years, when conditions are favourable, it reappears. So we can say that the Satpurush reveals his greatness and knowledge according to circumstances.

ME: Will you always watch over us?

KESHAV: (gently laughing) I'm watching... But it's not as simple as that. It only happens when we surrender our minds to the Guru and obey his commands without questioning him or harbouring the slightest doubt. But here we do the opposite! We raise questions in our mind. If you don't doubt God and Guru, even when they condemn our own ideas, only then will they watch over you.

ME: The Vachanamrut says: "By having intense love for the Satpurush, one is able to see one's own ātmā." How can we generate such love?

KESHAV: If we can realise its advantages, then we will generate stronger love. We are only ever attached to things that we feel are useful to us. Here, the benefit is liberation. Our ātmā benefits.

ME: What does it mean when we say that we should believe the Satpurush to be our true form?

KESHAV: Our true form is the ātmā, not the body. The Satpurush is our ātmā. We should believe his form to be ours. However, it will make no outward difference to our appearance, but still we should keep this one belief. We should do as the Satpurush tells us and maintain everlasting love towards him. If we want to realise ourselves as the ātmā, consider his form as ours and continue our efforts. His form is pure. There are no defects or traces of māyā in it. If we keep such conviction, the māyā within us is destroyed.

ME: How do we develop such conviction?

KESHAV: By constantly impressing this fault in our mind, it will become fixed. Then our defects with vanish. This body is not our form; it is temporary. The Satpurush's form is eternal, indestructible and peaceful. One who obeys his āgnā (spiritual commands) gains control of one's ātmā. We can only say we have realised his true form when we do what he says.

ME: I am happy sitting here and just having your darshan, that's all.

KESHAV: That's all there is. By looking at God and Guru, we experience tranquility.

ME: How would Pramukh Swami Maharaj describe his relationship with his guru, Shastriji Maharaj?

KESHAV: Shastriji Maharaj was the actual form of God. So, his relationship was that of God and his ideal devotee. He sought refuge in him, realising that he is the form of God. If we maintain such a relationship too, we will attain everlasting happiness and peace.

Being his, we should not attribute any faults to him or to his actions – see him as divine and flawless – and always follow his āgnā (spiritual commands).

ME: How do we maintain a constant link to God and Guru?

KESHAV: If we cannot keep God at the forefront in our mind, then all of our efforts are meaningless. Whether we are near the Guru or far away from him, we should always be aware of how we can please him. If he is pleased, we will progress. Those who have progressed on the spiritual path have done so because they have kept God and Guru at the forefront of their lives. No one ever progresses by their own efforts, intelligence or talents.

ME: You have an immense level of acceptance in your life. How have you developed the thought of God's all-doership in your live to such a level?

KESHAV: Everyone has to understand that! It is not for us alone to understand. Truly, we are not capable of doing anything – God is doing it all. Without his wish, we are not even capable of moving a dry leaf! It is wrong for us to take false pride that 'I did it', or, 'it was all because of me'. These are all false claims. To realise that without God nothing can happen, that he does everything, is a form of bhakti and a sign of our humility towards him. Live with radical humility and servitude – that is how our Gurus have lived. They have never preached anything else but radical humility and servitude.

ME: Why do you shower so much compassion upon us? We don't even deserve it!

KESHAV: God and Guru are merciful. They never look at the 'vicious' side. They only look towards our love. You have greater love and so he shows more compassion. The closer we become to him, the more he uses his love to draw us closer.

ME: What has been the happiest experience of your life?

KESHAV: Serving my Guru. Meeting the true Guru is happiness in itself!

ME: What do you regret in life.

KESHAV: By God's wish, we do our work. Everything happens according to his wishes. Even if we achieve nothing and everything falls apart, that too would be by his wish. [By maintaining such understanding] we have no regrets.

ME: What is the best thing in life?

KESHAV: God has given us this wonderful body. The best thing in life is to use it to do bhakti and satsang, as well as to keep faith in God and Guru.

ME: Has there ever been an incident that has caused you unhappiness?

KESHAV: No. There has never been such an incident. We constantly experience bliss.

ME: Hindu dharma stresses the importance of character and restraint of one's mind. Can you elaborate briefly?

KESHAV: Character and restraint are the main foundations of dharma. One is never fulfilled by indulgence, nor will one ever be. Just as pouring too much fuel onto a fire only smothers it, similarly over-indulgence only smothers our endeavours to attain God. We will never realise God in this way. Only character and restraint are the true ideals through which one can attain moksha.

ME: Can you briefly explain Bhagwan Swaminarayan's philosophical principles?

KESHAV: To realise oneself as the ātmā and offer bhakti to Paramātmā. Just as Radha-Krishna and Lakshmi-Narayan represent the dual philosophy of God and his ideal devotee, so does Akshar-Purushottam; meaning Swami and Narayan. This is an eternal philosophy. Akshar means to become brahmarup, and to then perform bhakti of Purushottam (God).

ME: Materialism is increasing in leaps and bounds. In light of this, what does the future hold for religion and dharma?

KESHAV: Materialism may be increasing, but what has always been the truth will always remain the truth. At present, it may seem that dharma is declining, but in the end, people will realise that science has not always been advantageous to us; it has only brought us closer to our own destruction (in reference to weaponry and war). Then they will turn back and revert to dharma. There is no reason for us to be disillusioned. The Guru's life will remain a constant source of inspiration; there will be no problems.

ME: What should one do to spiritually benefit from the Guru, at all times?

KESHAV: (jokingly) You'd have to always travel with him! But that is not possible now. Having a spiritual understanding is a very big thing. Once one gets this, all physical, mental and other such problems are solved. The total time Shastriji Maharaj spent with Bhagatji Maharaj was only three years. But he remained happy due to samjan. Spiritual understanding is what matters.

ME: Why should satsang take precedence in our life?

KESHAV: (empathetically) Everything else is hollow and temporary. Satsang is fulfilling. It is pure. It is pious. It solves all problems. By engaging in satsang, one's mind becomes focused, and applying it thereafter brings success. It is like sharpening a saw. By spending more time, we will benefit.

ME: Which is your favourite moral story?

KESHAV: Lindhiyo!

ME: Which negative trait do you despise the most?

KESHAV: Abhāv-avgun! Fault-finding!

ME: How do I know I will attain moksha?

KESHAV: Conviction. Pratiti. Akshardham is here.

ME: If Maharaj appeared in front of you right now, and granted you one wish, what would you ask for?

KESHAV: To give me the strength to live as dāsānudās (complete humility and servitude).

ME: Which quality should I aim to imbibe in my life?

KESHAV: Dāsānudās. That is it.

Shastra

[shaa-struh]

sacred scriptures

When the Chinese came to India with Xuanzang, they found a treasure of wisdom in the land through its culture, way of life, and scriptures. On their return back, aboard the ship, they took all of these scriptures and other antiques with them. The ship got damaged, and so, the weight of the ship needed to be lowered, otherwise it would sink. Xuanzang's men suggested they throw away the antiques, believing that as long as they survived, they'd be able to recreate them. They did it. But the weight aboard the ship still needed to be lowered. The men suggested throwing away the scriptures. Xuanzang immediately refused and said that these scriptures were not mere manuscripts or books, but within them, lay the future of China. He would not allow them to be thrown overboard, and he even went to the extent of saying that if weight needed to be lowered, he would jump overboard instead. A few of his men, inspired by this, sacrificed their lives and jumped overboard instead.

The Upanishads sing: "Lead me from ignorance to truth; from darkness into light; from death to immortality."[1] It is widely believed that the Vedic scriptures of India are literally the most ancient manuscripts of the world. They hold all of humanity's wisdom. It is said about the Mahabharat that what is within is elsewhere, and what is not within, cannot be found anywhere (i.e. the Mahabharat contains all the wisdom of life). The scriptures serve as a foundation to the most fundamental lessons of life, death and everything in between.

---

[1] Brihadaranyaka Upanishad 1.3.28

ME: What is the significance of scriptures?

KESHAV: In the modern day, mankind has progressed significantly in the outer sense. We've done so much for the body. The common man experiences more pleasures and comforts today than even Alexander the Great must have! But the problems that we face haven't gotten any less. Why do you think this is? Gandhi asked Tolstoy: "We want to make our country independent, please tell us what we should do?" Tolstoy replied: "Look towards your scriptures!" The scriptures contain all of the wisdom needed in life.

Montague said: "Book knowledge is mere nuisance. It may do for an ornament, but never for a foundation." Henry van Dyke said: "No doctrine, however high, however true, can make man happy until it has been translated into heart." The scriptures serve as a guide for us on how to purify our heart. It doesn't matter whether we believe it or not, you can't destroy the truth. You can hide it, but one day, it eventually comes out.

Because of the prevailing air of independence and freedom, we are losing our cultural roots and values. Pramukh Swami said: "No matter what, one should follow one's true values, cultivate greater faith in dharma, God, and his commands. The more one preserves spirituals values in one's life, the more the mind will be fortified, the better one's thoughts, and the more peace and progress one will attain." Maharaj says that only those who understand the message of the scriptures can be called humans!

ME: What is within is elsewhere, what is not within, is nowhere?

KESHAV: While narrating the Mahbharat to King Jannamejaya, Vaishampayana (one of Veda Vyas' disciples), says from the Mahabharat itself: "yad ihāsti tad anyatra yan nehāsti na tat kvacit."[2] This means: In matters pertaining to dharma (righteousness), artha (economics), kāma (desires), and moksha (liberation), whatever has been said here may be found elsewhere, but whatever is not found here does not exist anywhere else.

ME: What is the essence of the Shrimad Bhagavata Purana?

KESHAV: Maharaj asked this question to the scholar Dinanath Bhatt. Then he himself gave the answer, saying: 'prasangam-ajaram pasham-ātmanaha kavayo vidhuhu, sa eva sādhushu kruto moksha-dvāram-apāvrutam' (If a person maintains profound love towards the Ekantik Sādhu of God — the Guru — just as resolutely as he maintains profound love towards his own relatives, then the gateway to liberation is open for him).[3]

Without the Satpurush, moksha is impossible to attain. Thus, the essence of the Bhagavata is the Guru. When you develop this understanding, you win the world.

---

[2] Mahabharat 1.62.53
[3] Shrimad Bhagavata Purana 3.25.20

ME: What is the goal of human life.

KESHAV: Moksha. This should be understood with the essence and principles of Vyasji's deep reflection. Veda Vyas compiled so many scriptures... summarising them he said: 'ālodya sarva-shāstrāni vichārya cha punaha punaha, idam-ekam sunishpannam dhyeyo Nārayano Harihi' (After repeatedly reflecting on all of the scriptures, I have arrived at one principle conclusion – the goal of life is to attain God).

Even Tulsidas says that if one were to make hundreds and thousands in wealth, it is all useless without devotion towards God. Maharaj himself says in the last Vachanamrut: "Today I wish to say it as it is. There is nothing greater than to worship God."

In the Shrimad Bhagavata Purana, Rishabhdev says to his sons: "My dear boys, of all the living entities who have accepted material bodies in this world, one who has been awarded this human form should not work hard day and night simply for sense gratification. This is available to even dogs and hogs that eat stool. One should instead engage in penance and austerity to attain the divine position of devotional service. By such activity, one's heart is purified, and when one attains this position, he attains eternal, blissful life, which is transcendental to material happiness and which continues forever."[4] Even after this guidance, one of his sons, Bharatji, got attached to a deer and had to take another birth! Keep the goal clear. We are here for moksha.

---

[4] Shrimad Bhagavata Purana 5.5.1

ME: What does the Ramayan teach us?

KESHAV: Tolerance. It teaches us the true way to tolerate. Ramayan is made up of two words, 'ram' and 'ayan'; the word 'ayan' means 'way' or 'road', and so, Ramayan means 'the way of Rama', or, 'the road that Rama took'. Whether we take this literally or figuratively, both are of great importance. The Ramayan also teaches us the importance of tolerance, which is getting lower with each generation.

Napoleon used to say that impossible is a word only to be found in the dictionary of fools, but he was unable to maintain his own relationship with his wife! Lincoln failed thirteen times in getting to office, he even used to say that obstacles are stepping stones for him. Yet, he came to a point in his life where he wanted to commit suicide! Why? Lack of tolerance! Tolstoy had the same issues. The Ramayan teaches us how we should cultivate and flourish relationships with those around us. It also teaches us not to develop Manthrā-vrutti (mindset/attitude like that of Manthra).

When Rama was told he had to leave for the forest by his step-mother Kaikeyi, Rama went to meet Kaushalya. There, he said to her: "Mother! I have now acquired the kingdom of the jungle!" Tulsidas writes that in Kaushalya's mind a war begun; one between dharma and love. Kaushalya had realised what had happened. She could have easily persuaded Dashratha too. Tulsidas then writes that it was like a snake had swallowed a mouse. She was in a dilemma of what to do.

In the end she chose to stand by dharma and didn't let her emotions rule over her. She differentiated between *what* was right and *who* was right. If they all went by *who* is right, that would have been for the sake of justice and would have been self-centred. Instead, by going with *what* is right, they stuck by duty, obligation and encompassed others. Keeping 'what is right' in mind, Kaushalya said to Rama: "Do as your father has said, that is correct." She put her personal preferences and love aside for the sake of dharma. Pride is about *who* is right, humility is about *what* is right.

Sitaji focused on what is right too. She didn't object once in her life. She *always* supported Rama. We cannot wallow in self-pity. We, as humans, love to sing of our own misery. It almost feels like a competition to us! But this doesn't solve any of our issues, does it? Kaushalya stood by her principles, not her emotions. Sitaji did the same. The whole family went by *what* is right. Tulsidas writes in the Ramcharitmanas that a person who is not enticed by the sense pleasures, who is above anger and free of greed, he is equal to Rama.

Always look towards the resolution of the problem, do not focus on what *has* happened, otherwise you will get tied up in the cycle of that. The brother of Rama, Shatrugna, wanted to kill Manthra but Kaikeyi tried to stop him. Bharat stopped him too and said: "You want to kill Manthra for your ego, but I want to kill Kaikeyi! She is the cause of all of this. Yet, I control myself because I know Rama won't be pleased, and if Rama isn't pleased, then there is no point in living." Bharat had samjan. We must always focus on that which pleases God and Guru. Maharaj said: "Dashratha had greater love for his queen than his own son and so he sent Rama, who was not at fault, to the forest. He did not have even the slightest compassion towards his son." In [Vachanamrut Gadhada] II-11, Maharaj says that all karmas (actions) become a form of bhakti (devotion) when we continuously ask ourselves if in what we're doing, will God and Guru be pleased? This is a technique. This is what the scriptures teach us.

ME: What should we understand as the essence of philosophy?

KESHAV: In [Vachanamrut Gadhada] II-3, Maharaj distinguishes between Brahma and Parabrahma. Brahma is not the same as Parabrahma. To believe God to always have a form is itself upāsanā[5]. The more you contemplate on your attainment, the more humility you will develop. It is important to affirm that you are not the body, not just the fact that you are the ātmā, otherwise you will believe the ātmā to be the body itself!

We never develop oneness with Parabrahma, we develop oneness with Brahma. Once we develop that oneness with Brahma, we become *like* Brahma, and only then do we become worthy of worship and service of Parabrahma. Today, Akshar-Purushottam is one. Within Akshar, Purushottam forever resides. Today, we must understand Pramukh Swami to be the very form of Parabrahma.

---

[5] the philosophical understanding of the nature of God as well as the mode of worship of God; sometimes synonymous with bhakti

How can one ever find a black cat in a dark room? You can't! You need a guide. Similarly, on the spiritual path, one needs a guide too. You cannot tread this path of one's own accord. That is why we have a guru.

Maharaj himself has said that intense love towards the Satpurush is everything.[6] This is the essence of all philosophy, spiritual endeavour and all belief. It is all that needs to be done on the path of moksha.

ME: What is vivek?

KESHAV: To know one's base natures is vivek (spiritual discretion) and to dissolve those base natures is param vivek (highest form of spiritual discretion). Vachanamrut [Gadhada] III-24, I-6 and I-16. Through associating with the great Sādhu, one develops vivek. They are able to distinguish between the ātmā and non-ātmā.

ME: What is wisdom?

KESHAV: Vachanamrut [Gadhada] II-24 and III-38. The last birth. [Vachanamrut Gadhada] III-39: ātmā and Paramātmā.

---

[6] Vachanamrut Vartal 11

ME: Are all the answers in the Vachanamrut?

KESHAV: Yogiji Maharaj gave us all the knowledge of the Vachanamrut from his life... One who understands [Vachanamruts] Kariyani 8 and Gadhada II-7 will see Akshardham manifest before their eyes. One should read [Vachanamrut Gadhada] I-17 daily. The essence of all scriptures is to realise the true form of God. When one understands [Vachanamrut] Loya 12, then one understands the glory of all.. One should read and talk about [Vachanamrut] Loya 17. Master [Vachanamrut] Kariyani 10, read it three times and introspect on the last line.

Maharaj says: "I have read and understood *all* the words of *all* the scriptures on this planet, and I conclude that the essence of it all is to serve the Sant through thought, word and deed. This is the lifeline."[7]

ME: I read the scriptures but feel no peace or happiness within. What should I do to destroy my inner enemies and experience satisfaction?

KESHAV: Read. Contemplate. Put it into practice. You cannot do it of your own accord. Spiritual progress is only to be had through the association of the Guru. He is the only one who can direct.

---

[7] Vachanamrut Gadhada III-28

LESSONS FROM THE RAMAYAN

The story of the Ramayan is full of conflict. Why? Because life is full of conflicts. It is only the dead who have no conflict. Conflict exists within the body to the most minute detail with white blood cells and pathogens, all the way up to the global scale with war. When we look towards the story of Rama, we see how he was instantaneously reduced from becoming king to a beggar. His entire life was full of conflict too.

The majority of conflict in life is illusory. To maintain discretion, we must identify our conflicts instead of simply imagining or proliferating them. When Hanuman burnt Lanka, he sank into sadness because he remembered that Sitaji was also in Lanka! He kept thinking and proliferating the situation in his mind, to the extent that he wanted to commit suicide! He thought: "Without Sita, there is no Rama; without Rama, there is no Lakshmana; without Lakshmana, there is no Bharat!" And he kept on ruminating. That is why we mustn't just imagine our conflicts, but check first. Pain creates conflicts.

Rama didn't brand or stamp Vibhishana (the brother of Ravana) due to his association. He didn't complicate conflict. Dharma sets the fine line for how we should behave and act within this world. We must stay within limits and boundaries, whether that is emotional, moral or social limits. Sitaji crossed the boundary and she suffered. Similarly, boundaries exist for each and every one of us, but should we choose to cross them, then we are bound to suffer.

The army of Vānaras built a bridge from India to Lanka – united through Rama. Bridges are built across nations when we first build them amongst ourselves; when we come together united with harmony. When it was time for Ravana to be cremated, his brother Vibhishana, didn't want to cremate him. This is when Rama taught him to forgive and forget. Dharma is more important than emotions. The best way to defeat your enemy is to turn him into your friend. You are not the centre of the world, but you are the centre of *your* world.

We learn from King Dashratha's life how we can all fall prey to our base instincts. He was infatuated by Kaikeyi, but deep down he never really wanted Rama to leave. Dashratha was not dutiful for three reasons: his desires, he couldn't maintain indifference, and he wasn't open or honest either. Valmiki writes that he was enveloped by lust and desire. He didn't stick by *what* was right. Why didn't Dashrartha say no to granting Kaikeyi's wish? Doesn't it make you wonder? He was enveloped by his base instincts. There is a Dashratha within each one of us. We seek to please everyone around us, but rarely do we think about pleasing God and Guru. Seek only to please them and you will live a peaceful life. Rama was in front of his family, yet people didn't recognise him for who he was. It is said that he lived for 12,000 years. Rama is the ideal of tolerance and forgiveness. Upon returning to Ayodhya, he bowed to Kaikeyi *first*. The one who bows, even in front of those who've harmed him, is loved by all.

LESSONS FROM THE MAHABHARAT

The Mahabharat teaches us that wars begin in the minds of the individual. Each one of us is fighting a war within our mind. The Pandavas and Kauravas lived together, but they did so only for property, status and wealth. The Kauravas were jealous of the virtuous qualities that came naturally to the Pandavas. They could not tolerate the praises and positive qualities of the Pandavas. When we compare ourselves to those around us, the war in our mind only proliferates.

Dritharashtra also felt self-pity because he was blind and because he didn't inherit the throne. Like many parents do today, he forced his unfulfilled wishes onto his son from the very beginning. Throughout history, even families have been killed for empires and wealth. As good as Yudhisthir may have been, and despite his belief that compassion was the highest dharma, he was addicted to gambling. Addictions afflict all of us – whether that be to substances or to certain behaviours – we are all addicted to something.

The Mahabharat shares the essence of dharma in its own words: "What is not good for me cannot be cast upon by me unto others. What is not good for me would not be good for others also, because others are like me in every respect."[8] Ignorance is to

[8] Mahabharat 5.15.17

believe the body to be your true form. Ego is the very form of infatuation. Without God and Guru, one cannot rid of their ego. The root of all defects (dosha) is ahamkāra (ego). The Guru alone can take us above ahamkāra.

In the Mahabharat of our lives, we all need to become Partha (Arjun). There is no devotee like Arjun. He developed complete refuge and conviction in God. Bhishma, on the bed of arrows, asked Shri Krishna why he had to suffer if he has not done anything wrong in his life. Maybe this question is retrospective of ourselves. But Krishna told him how he *chose* to stay quiet when Draupadi was being stripped. Silence is not *always* the answer, especially when it comes to the subtle art of dharma.

Ultimately, the Mahabharat teaches us how to fight our mind, so that we can remain stable and at peace amidst all circumstances in life. It teaches us to have complete faith in God and Guru, living according to their wishes alone.

Sharnagati

[shur-naa-gut-ee]

total surrender or refuge

As a foetus, we seek the refuge of a nurturing mother. As a child, when we fall and stumble, we seek the refuge of a caring father. As a growing teenager, we seek the refuge of our friends and family, who we confide in and hope that we can trust. But, unfortunately, as we grow older in today's world, we are becoming more and more distant. In reality, we feel more alone today than ever before. So, where do we seek refuge? Where can we feel the true love of a parent, a friend or family?

ME: What is the need for prayer?

KESHAV: Prayer is to derive strength from God and Guru. Shastriji Maharaj said: "If you remember God once, he remembers you a thousand times over!" Hellen Keller said: "No prayer goes unheard." Draupadi prayed to Krishna and he protected her. During the Apollo mission, the entire nation of the USA resorted to prayer. It is the most powerful tool in the most challenging of times. But we should never use it as a spare wheel! Pramukh Swami said: "In prayer, it's not how well you arrange your words, but it's how well you arrange your heart that counts."

ME: What is the need for refuge in God?

KESHAV: Life is an ocean of pain and happiness, where even the strongest cannot swim with success. It is impossible to swim the vast ocean with one's own strength, but with faith in God, it is possible. In [Vachanamrut Gadhada] I-3, Muktanand Swami asks: "The scriptures have described innumerable spiritual endeavours to please God; but amongst them all, which one is so powerful that it alone earns as much pleasure of God as is earned by performing *all* spiritual endeavours combined?"

In short, he asks Maharaj what endeavour encompasses all endeavours. Maharaj replies: "Accepting the firm refuge of God is the single, greatest endeavour amongst all spiritual endeavours for pleasing God. That refuge, though, must be extremely firm and without any flaws." You need unflinching faith in God.

If you surrender to God in totality, God looks after you. One must let go of the ego to totally surrender to God. The ego is the cause of all misery and suffering. Maharaj even said that there is no greater *taste* than the ego. Aham (I-ness) and mamatva (my-ness) is itself māyā, it is at the core of the kāran (causal) body. Drapaudi kept firm refuge when it was needed, so she was protected.

ME: Do we seek refuge in the Guru?

KESHAV: Yes. Sometimes we think that such statements are there just to convince us. We feel as if we are coaxed into believing such things. This is a big misconception. The Guru's words are true. He uplifts society. He helps us transcend our mundane existence, not just that, the Guru emancipates us from the aimless cycle of birth and death. It sounds nonsensical, but it is not. The Guru has truly realised God, and thus speaks from experience. He is enlightened and detached from all forms of ignorance. He is never enticed by the temptations of this world. He is incredibly virtuous. He is not an ordinary monk. His life reflects a solid legacy. After attaining him, there is nothing more to attain.

Remain fulfilled and maintain faith. Akshardham is here. That which we wish to attain at the end of this life, we have attained right here, right now. If one has such unflinching faith, one can remain steady in all walks of life. But you can't be heedless. Work hard and imbibe this wisdom. It comes to one automatically when the principle is applied. You become spiritually strong. You must find fulfilment from within. You must remain at peace and indifferent to the ups and downs of this world.

Following commands are important too. Once when Yogiji Maharaj was asked what commands are, he said: "To follow any wish of his [the Guru] – big or small; to believe one's ātmā to be Brahma; and to not be affected by negative words. When these three are imbibed, we can be said to have sought refuge."

ME: Doesn't God take care of everyone though?

KESHAV: It is true that God takes care of everyone, but we fail to comprehend this because we are drowned in the delusion of our own selfish viewpoints. When all of this creation is God's, won't he protect his creation?

ME: If one seeks refuge in God, is he freed for all past sins?

KESHAV: God is merciful. He forgives us all for our past sins. However, after seeking his shelter, if we continue to knowingly sin then we must bear the consequences. Only one who has no devotion in his heart sins purposefully. He never seeks refuge in God, nor does he believe in the power of God, and so, he just continues sinning. A true devotee would instantly feel guilt upon committing even the smallest mistake. One who continually sins eventually suffers from his own ignorance.

Maharaj says that as long as one acts wilfully, one does not rise above the jiva state. There is no greater moksha than to act according to the wish of God. The central message of all scriptures is this.

ME: Wherever we look, we see evil flourishing. Those who stand up for righteousness and justice are often viciously put down and made to suffer. In such circumstances, how can one be expected to keep faith in dharma?

KESHAV: Death will always do its job of spreading hardship and suffering. In this age of Kali, those who are bad are made out to be great. But be sure, in the end, truth always triumphs. Bearing that in mind, one should always live one's life according to dharma. Those who are wrong, for a time may seem to be famous and influential in society, but when their time comes, they all fall, after which no one even remembers their names.

220 • VINAY SUTARIA

Money obtained by deceit and cheating won't help a man sleep at night. On the other hand, a person who earns his food with good, honest labour, even if he only gets a little to eat, it will taste sweet to him, and that sweetness will reach deep into his heart.

ME: What is the shortcut to pleasing you?

KESHAV: (signals haircut whilst laughing)

ME: My conviction and faith is still not firm. Why?

KESHAV: It takes time. When one takes a course of medicine, it works gradually. In the same way, patiently continue on the spiritual path and maintain faith. The more you apply [this principle], the greater your conviction will become. Maharaj says: "There is no greater endeavour than to develop love towards the Sādhu, who is greater than even the body and family. If one develops the same love towards God and his Sādhu, as one has for one's family and relatives, then one instantly transcends the world."

सार:

Sar

[saar]
essence

Today, we are drowned in information. There is so much out there, that we can't filter out what we need. The answers we all seek often need to be simplified, into the essence, so that we can comprehend, contemplate and implement them into our own lives. It is only through Keshav that the essence comes forth as it is.

ME: What does one need to understand?

KESHAV: God is the all-doer. There is nothing else to understand other than this. If one truly understands satsang, then one would forgo all pleasures of this world. You don't dissolve pleasures, you dissolve attachments. One who indulges in the pleasures of the physical body is a pauper, no matter how great he may be. However, when a person behave as the ātmā, he is of a different calibre altogether. Only one who believes themselves to be the ātmā is truly free.

Yogi Bapa asked me to memorise [Vachanamrut Gadhada] III-11 when I first came to him. Don't find flaws in anyone. We tend to run to the places and people where our ego gets fuelled. We must stop this. Not seeing one's own flaws is a major flaw in itself. The ego is a terrorist within! Don't let it infiltrate you, otherwise it will destroy you. Muktanand Swami says: "Erase the 'I' and God is near." Mutual love, mutual understanding, divine vision – that is what we need to cultivate.

The ultimate goal of life is moksha. If we go to Mumbai for some work, do we tell others we're there for food, sleep? Of course not! The main thing must always remain the main thing. Pramukh Swami also said that to attain peace in life, you must understand God's greatness. In [Vachanamrut] Vartal 4, Maharaj says: "Through serving the Sant by thought, word and deed, nothing else is left to be done." The essence of all the scriptures is to serve the Sant.

ME: What is māyā?

KESHAV: The influence of māyā can be seen manifest in everything mobile and immobile. Māyā is incomprehensible and formless; it is filled with countless joys and miseries. It is known as inanimate, illusory and full of misery. Infinite universes are under the control of māyā. Infinite types of barriers and disturbances reside within it. It causes fluctuation of thoughts, ego and attachment, and it is the cause of countless types of joy and misery.

On the spiritual path, an evil mind can be regarded as the very form of māyā. Just as the clouds hide the sun, māyā covers the ātmā. That māyā, in the form of ignorance, has made everyone helpless. The jiva does not know that this ignorance is the root cause of its misery, and so, it believes that misery is joy. To free the jiva from this primordial ignorance is a great strength that is inherent to God and his Sādhu.

ME: What is sat (real) and what is asat (illusion)?

KESHAV: Sat is the ātmā, sat is the non-ātmā (the body and the mind). To see with divinity is to see things as above māyā. If you are brahmarup, you will see others as brahmarup too. This is satsang. We must also get rid of our ignorance. What is that ignorance? I-ness and my-ness, affection towards those we are attached with – this all seems real to us, but it isn't.

ME: What gives us misery and what gives us peace?

KESHAV: The root of all misery is the mind. If you sway from dharma, there is only misery. Living within dharma gives one peace. Maharaj says: "If we understand greatness, we experience happiness continuously. If we understand this, we experience astonishment all of the time."[1] Shankaracharya also said: "Birth is full of pain; old age is full of miseries; woman[2] is again and again the source of misery and pain. In this ocean of sansār, there is nothing but grief. So wake up! Wake up!"

You only progress when you learn to adjust in life – both mentally and physically. Let go of your predispositions. Adjust to others. Tolerate. There is no greater status than that of tolerance. It is about knowing yourself. You may know everything in the world, but if

---

[1] Vachanamrut Gadhada I-24 and I-78
[2] and vice-versa

you don't know yourself, it is all a waste! What does it matter if you know everything in the world, but you fail to know and realise yourself? Realise yourself to be *nothing*, and everyone to be *above* you. This is what Uddhavji did with the Gopis... he didn't ask to sit with God, but to sit with the devotees of God. He became the servant of the servant!

ME: What is the need for codes of conduct and āgnā?

KESHAV: They draw the lines of dharma. If you take the correct dosage of medicine, it's fine, but if you take a dose exceeding the limit, it can be poisonous – in the same way, these set the limits for us.

ME: How do we see God?

KESHAV: God cannot be seen just like that. You have to keep faith in the words of the Guru and exert yourself spiritually. I can see God within my Guru. There is nothing more to be said. God may come before us in any form he pleases to!"

After visiting Niagara Falls, Pramukh Swami wrote in a letter to the youth of London: "No wonder in this world can equal the three wonders: Maharaj, Swami and Yogiji Maharaj. After seeing them, nothing else remains to be seen."

ME: What is the essence of dharma?

KESHAV: Dharma is that which spreads love for one another. We are all ātmās, so we are all inherently divine. The scriptures say: 'vayam amrutasya putrāhā' (we are all children of the eternal). Dharma is only one – humanity and sadāchār (purity in all actions). Without dharma, even bhakti, jnān and vairāgya cannot lead to moksha.

ME: What is swadharma?

KESHAV: To follow one's own observances with dedication. To follow the observances as per one's varnāshram[3] and to develop unwavering fidelity.

ME: What is jnān?

KESHAV: Pramukh Swami believed jnān should not merely be hollow or empty words, but it should be translated into a unique life full of joy and wedded to morality. Renounce self-pity. Only when one is strict upon oneself is one saved from self-pity. Yogiji Maharaj often said: "Crush one's senses and mind. They must quake with fear!" He also said that if one does not keep negligence and infatuation, then it is said that one has unshakeable knowledge. The essence of all spiritual wisdom is to know yourself as the ātmā.

---

[3] referring to the four stages of life according to Hindu belief

ME: What is bhakti?

KESHAV: To continuously see everything as divine is bhakti.

ME: What is faith?

KESHAV: To not doubt that which God and Guru say.

ME: What is introspection?

KESHAV: To do as God and Guru say is itself introspection.

ME: What is true austerity?

KESHAV: To fight the mind. To do what the mind wants is inferior. To do what the Sant says is superior. There is no bondage in that and one experiences peace.

ME: How can one attain the knowledge of the ātmā?

KESHAV: The ātmā is lustrous. When one dies, one element leaves the body – that is the ātmā. Realisation of *this* is the knowledge of ātmā. One can attain such realisation by associating with the Satpurush.

ME: When will the earth be destroyed.

KESHAV: That we won't witness. Realise yourself as Akshar and you will experience jnān pralay (destruction through knowledge). Creation, sustenance and destruction of this cosmos are time dependent, and time (kāl) acts as God directs.

ME: How is world peace possible?

KESHAV: If people become more religious and all religions help one another, world peace can be established.

ME: Will honesty and truth ever succeed in this world?

KESHAV: Only they will be victorious! Only through them will we attain peace. Even if we only have a hut as a home, we will still be content. There is nothing greater than being at peace within the heart.

ME: When can we say that we have been successful in life?

KESHAV: Life is only worthwhile if we do good deeds and walk on the path towards God. The reasons for success are purity in life and faith in God.

ME: What is the purpose of life?

KESHAV: The purpose of life is to do bhakti of God. Of course, we need to fulfil our social obligations towards our family and to society, but life's primary goal is to engage in satsang and to attain liberation of the ātmā. There is nothing in this entire universe comparable to bhakti.

ME: What is the most amazing thing in this world?

KESHAV: That someday we will have to leave this world and yet we can't let go of our attachment to our prosperity and possessions. Devanand Swami writes: "Those who were clever, intelligent and had much wealth and prosperity have all gone, leaving everything behind." Another amazing thing is that we have met God and Guru. We have attained that which we would have never attained on our own accord. This is the highest level of grace!

ME: Who was I in my past life?

KESHAV: First ask yourself, 'Who am I right now? Why was I born?' If you don't understand that, what is the use of knowing about the past or the future? You don't even know who you are right now and yet you wish to know who you were in your past life. Know yourself as you are, and you shall know everything.

ME: What should one do to be a good human?

KESHAV: To be even human one should have compassion, honesty, non-violence, discipline and niyams firm in one's life. If we can make such distinctions then we will be human, otherwise we are no different to animals. No matter what faith one practises, whichever caste or community one belongs to, if one is not moral then one is not a human being. A person's life speaks for itself.

It is said: 'dayā dharma kā mul he, pāp mul abhimān' (compassion is the foundation of dharma; ego is the foundation of sin). Righteous living is purity of diet, purity of thought, and purity in one's social dealings. If these three are pure, that is righteous living. Dharma is true wealth. All faiths teach that a life of pure character, that is free from addiction, leads to happiness. The way to become pure is through a strong positive desire and trust. Without that, true detachment does not arise. Knowing the four types of pralay (destruction) leads to detachment.

ME: It seems like society is heading in the wrong direction. How can we uplift the minds of people?

KESHAV: (laughing gently) That is why we preach and travel. No matter how great the temptations we face, we should never be lured towards them. We do not want a nice car or a big house, we only want to serve society. If we keep such intentions, we won't have any problems. We should live a simple, content and pure life. The more we increase our wants and needs, the more we will experience discontent. Life is not meant for the enjoyment of pleasures, they are available to even animals! Yes, you should live and work in society, but only enough to meet your needs. But our goal is not to attach ourselves to worldly pleasures.

ME: In today's materialistic world, the younger generation is blinded. Because of that, all forms of progress are being hampered. How can we overcome this?

KESHAV: Today's social climate is indeed evil. Parents know it and even we know it. But only by realising the greatness of spirituality will we be able to restrain our mind from being lured. We should have a firm conviction from within that we want to reap the benefits of spirituality. By keeping the company of the pure, one indeed becomes pure. If we realise ourselves as the ātmā, then we will have no problems.

ME: But at a young age, we all have high ambitions...

KESHAV: [interrupts] In this world, ambitions have never lasted and will never last. The only ambition which is of any use is to engage in bhakti and to please God and Guru. We should also have an ambition to be good. In whichever field one is in, one should always be honest and honourable. Live according to the rules and regulations. We will only be of any use if we try to be good, and through trying, we will find peace.

ME: How did you progress so much?

KESHAV: If we remain smaller than everyone, we become bigger [in the eyes of God]. But those who try to become bigger than the rest, only end up becoming the smallest [i.e. Inferior]. We should never try to get ahead at the expense of another. Those who help others help themselves.

ME: What expectations do you have of me?

KESHAV: What should I expect? That you massage my hands or my head? No! I don't expect that, nor do I expect everyone to become a sādhu either, but you should at least become a good devotee. Study hard, serve the people and the country, be honourable, honest, and live according to niyam-dharma, so that whichever field you are in, you won't have any problems. We want to build a good society; one that has no corruption and only honourable people who do honest, hard work. Condition yourself to be like that.

ME: Many become disillusioned in times of failure. What should one do?

KESHAV: Those who try to get ahead by their own efforts, without finding a true Guru, will become disillusioned in times of failure. But if they had a Guru – a guide – then they would derive strength and inspiration and find solutions to their problems. Secondly, people fail because of their base nature. Man degenerates because of his infatuation to worldly pleasures. If we can realise our true form, control our senses, and believe ourselves to be the ātmā, then what problems are there? If we can harness our senses and seek refuge in the true Guru, then all problems dissipate.

ME: What is the highest level of acceptance?

KESHAV: Gunatitanand Swami says: 'mānav jāne me karyu, kartal duo koi; ādaryā adhurā rahe, Hari kare so hoi' (man thinks he has done it, but the doer is someone else; the task remains incomplete, whatever God wills happens).

ME: Why is bhakti given so much predominance?

KESHAV: The Shrimad Bhagavata Purana says: "It is completely inappropriate if one possesses knowledge of Paramātmā, the remover of ignorance, yet does not possess bhakti."[4]

The jiva acquires strength from the following three endeavours: exceptionally intense service, deep faith, and devotion with an understanding of God's greatness. Such strength is not attained even if one is able to discriminate between the ātmā and the body, and even if one behaves as ātmārup.

---

[4] Shrimad Bhagavata Purana 1.5.12

ME: What is sānkhya and what is yoga?

KESHAV: Knowledge is sānkhya; meditation is yoga. The state of tranquility is when the vruttis (emanations of the senses and mind) of the senses are introverted and reside in the region of the heart.

ME: Who will be victorious?

KESHAV: One who has dharma-niyam (righteous living within the codes of conduct) and firm faith in God will be victorious.

ME: Will my ego be dissolved?

KESHAV: If you want it to be, it will be. If you persevere, you can achieve anything. If you want to please Pramukh Swami, you will put everything aside to do so. One should never have an ego about one's own qualities either. In every endeavour, ego is the greatest enemy. No matter how intelligent one is, humility should *always* be maintained.

ME: What is the purpose of *my* life?

KESHAV: To attain God.

ME: What is moksha?

KESHAV: The worldly path is different from the path of moksha. Moksha is associated with one's ātmā, whereas the worldly path is related to one's body. Moksha means to give up one's ego (aham) and [worldly] attachments (mamatva), which is itself māyā, and to then engage in bhakti.

Ego and attachments are the two poisons; they are the very form of māyā. If you get rid of them, divine bliss can be experienced right here on earth.

ME: What is brahmavidhyā?

KESHAV: To see all as divine. Bhagatji said that the essence of brahmavidhya is to win over the mind. That is it.

ME: How can one purify one's heart?

KESHAV: By associating with the guru. Through pleasing God and Guru. One should enter the domain of soul-power and the power of God's glory. Then, many problems will be solved. Physical power, intellectual power and other powers are of no use [in solving acute issues].

ME: How does one attain God?

KESHAV: By giving up the resolves of one's mind and obeying *his* words.

ME: There are countless talks relating to God. Can you tell me about him briefly?

KESHAV: Gunatitanand Swami has said: "We are born for two reasons – to become ātmārup[5] and to attach ourselves to Purushottam." When the devotees of Kathiawar told Maharaj: "You are ours and we are yours," Maharaj replied: "At the end of the day, this is the one understanding everyone needs to cultivate." After all spiritual endeavour, penance, austerity, contemplation, or reading, this is the one thing we have to understand – God is ours and we are God's.

ME: If there is a God, then why do so many people suffer?

KESHAV: Man's actions are such that because of them, he experiences joy and pain. God does not create hardships, we create them. We get into difficulties because of our own weaknesses. If you are diabetic, and you still eat sugary foods, you will suffer right? Our scriptures tell us what we should and shouldn't do, if we choose not to follow them, whose fault is that? The government has made a law that one should stop at a red light. If we don't stop, we will obviously suffer the consequences. Codes of conduct are

---

[5] the form of ātmā; synonymous to brahmarup, or, ātmārup

devised so that we can live life conveniently and peacefully. That is why God has commanded us to follow the scriptures. If we don't practice niyams (codes of conduct) in our lives, we will be miserable. Maharaj himself says that the extent to which the boundaries established by the great are transgressed is the extent to which misery is experienced. That is not God's fault. Niyams are essential. God has devised 'laws' and niyams for our benefit, but if we don't follow them, then we are only creating our own problems. Dharma doesn't restrict, it uplifts. It is not God who creates hardships for man, it is man who creates hardships for man.

ME: People who aren't spiritual, or don't believe in God, still progress...

KESHAV: That's true, but one who obtains wealth by immoral means never experiences peace at heart. He may have an aeroplane and he may travel around the world in it, or he may have an expensive car, a big house and everything, but he won't be happy at heart. We have met millionaires and billionaires, most of whom don't feel peace at heart... It all remains superficial.

Outwardly some may appear happy, but inwardly, do they feel spiritually fulfilled? Although we have never hurt others, by God's wish we may face hardships, but this is only so that we can become pure. By following dharma, we can attain harmony in our families, our society, and in our country.

ME: How fortunate are we?

KESHAV: Having attained God and Guru we have benefited greatly. This is for the benefit of the soul. All other benefits are transitory. Material prosperity, fame and power are just worldly benefits. They are temporary – until we live – they are short-lived. God and Guru's presence is felt here – right now – and hereafter too. God and Guru *always* look after us. Pleasure and pain are inevitable, but our faith and devotion should never sway. Have an unwavering attitude. Our mind tends to falter at times. One *must* pass the test of faith. I pray to God that everyone is always protected and that all are blessed with good health, happiness, peace and prosperity in all that they do.

ME: How should we develop acceptance and remain at peace?

KESHAV: There is a saying that what happens to you is ten percent, and how you take it is ninety percent. Incidents will occur in life, but it all comes down to how you perceive them. If you feel bitter and devastated by events, then you will not experience happiness. We all accept God to be the all-doer, but sometimes, due to uncertainty, we do so half-heartedly.

Bhagatji Maharaj used to accept all situations with joy. He was resolute. He realised it was a test of faith by God and Guru. We should learn from Bhagatji. Not because of his wisdom and knowledge alone, but because it is the absolute truth – God is the all-doer.

We need to cultivate and apply this wisdom into our daily life. The stronger your faith, the greater the sense of freedom. If you take things positively, you will naturally become happier and more peaceful.

ME: What is the essence of all the scriptures?

KESHAV: To have firm refuge [or faith] in God. There should be no lapses in that. One who remains unmoved experiences peace. Faith is the strongest of all endeavours, there is nothing comparable to it.

ME: How does one remain cheerful on the spiritual path?

KESHAV: By perceiving all to be divine. It is written: "You obtained wealth obsessing that 'it is only mine'. Actually, not even a grain's worth is yours." Why obsess over things being ours or not? We should relish in the happiness of attaining God, not from the happiness that we amass from money or assets.

Money and power are the two main causes of conflict. In the desire for wealth, power and lust, people forget their dharma. It's not wrong to strive. We have to do these things to sustain ourselves. In fact, the greatest source of energy comes from taking pride in one's work and actions. However, true joy and bliss will only be felt from the attainment of God. Never feel that you are inferior or lesser than another.

Don't wallow in self-pity either. One who is faithful, stands with their head high. Always remain joyful and strong. Never be numbed due to your circumstances in this world.

ME: When can it be said that complete satsang and wisdom is imbibed?

KESHAV: When one believes that he who we wish to attain after death, has been attained right here, and knowing this, when one diverts one's attention away from the world, only then can it be said that one has imbibed satsang completely.

Yogi Bapa said that in complete wisdom, one sees everyone and everything with complete divinity. One acts in a way where everyone feels at peace in their presence. One who develops such wisdom, experiences peace within and allows others to feel such peace too. When one develops ultimate wisdom, they feel at ease within.

ME: What is the state of Brahma?

KESHAV: Whilst understanding the greatness of the manifest form and developing the thought of divinity, when one understands that the form in Akshardham and the one on earth to be one, then one's jiva has attained the supreme knowledge and state.

ME: What are the qualities of this state?

KESHAV: When praises and insults appear as one, that is the state of Brahma.

ME: Where can one's heart find tranquility?

KESHAV: Tulsidas has said: "You may look in paradise, on earth, or even in hell, but nowhere will you find happiness. For happiness can only be found at the feet of God or his chosen Sādhu." Only God and Guru can give us peace. If you keep God in your heart, tranquility will pervade. By realising God to be the all-doer, one experiences tranquility.

ME: What do you experience in your life?

KESHAV: Peace.

ME: Do you ever get stressed?

KESHAV: No. [I believe] God to be the all-doer.

ME: Do you experience the bliss of Akshardham?

KESHAV: Continuously. Always.

ME: What words should we use to philosophically introduce you?

KESHAV: Param Ekāntik Sant.

ME: And now?

KESHAV: Understand [Vachanamrut Gadhada] I-16. You will understand everything. Believe one's ātmā to be Brahma. The body and ātmā are separate. Read and introspect on [Vachanamrut] Sarangpur 1 and Sarangpur 11. Master Vachanamrut Vartal 11. Believe the Sādhu to be your very own soul. Love him alone. That is the only way to self-realisation. That is the only way to God-realisation. That is the essence of all essence..

ME: Who was Pramukh Swami Maharaj?

KESHAV: Parabrahma manifest.

THE ROAD AHEAD

As I was writing, again and again, I came across new findings and research that further expanded on the topics of this book. It made me realise that this journey is still in its beginning steps, and there is a whole lot more to unfold. I hope that you continue to join me on this journey.

Of course, we have a hand to guide us, but nevertheless, the path must be forged by us alone. This is how we discover true bliss and joy. I hope that these conversations have inspired you as much as they've inspired me. Believe me, this is just the start of something new. Continue to tread this path. Maintain faith in God and Guru. Stay strong. Stay brave. I'm here to support you, encourage you, and if you ever want to talk, reach out to me **@the.keshav.way** on Instagram.

In the most divine land on this planet, whilst remembering God and Guru, I offer my deepest prayers for you and your loved ones. May you truly connect to Keshav and experience bliss here and now.

Vinay Sutaria
13 September 2022
Ahmedabad, India

ACKNOWLEDGEMENTS

I offer my sincere gratitude and heartfelt prayers to HH Pramukh Swami Maharaj (1921-2016), whose life and teachings have been the foundation of how I wish to live my life. My spiritual guru, HH Mahant Swami Maharaj (b. 1933), who has been a constant inspiration and example in living a life of humility, integrity, divinity and perfected character. Without their blessings, love, support, and guidance, these conversations would never have been possible. I am eternally grateful to them.

I'd also like to extend special thanks to the Swamis of Neasden Temple, as well as the various swamis and scholars of BAPS across the globe, for their continuous insights, guidance and support in ensuring clarity and authenticity. I also thank them for providing guidance in my times of need and confusion. A special thanks to Stuti Patel for the illustrations and drawings for this book. Thank you to all the silent editors and proofreaders, who came forward and offered to read and critique the manuscript, on top of dealing with my own endless streams of edits, reviews and changes to the text! A shoutout goes to Saagar at Prime for the cover design and formatting. Finally, I express my gratitude to you for the love, support and blessings that you have given me – to every one of my readers, family, friends, well-wishers, and supporters. It is because of your enthusiasm, zeal and love, that I even had the opportunity to put a pen to the paper.

ABOUT THE AUTHOR

Vinay Sutaria is a young, budding IT professional by day, and an avid reader and writer by night. Born and raised in the UK, he graduated with a degree in Computer Science from the University of Leicester. Vinay is a well-versed speaker and is known for his powerful and inspirational oratory skills. He refers to himself as a lifelong learner, who loves to share ideas and thoughts with others. Vinay is also a member of the BABCP (British Association for Behavioural and Cognitive Psychotherapies). He regularly travels to India, where he gains new experiences and insights into philosophy, science, sociology and life. Vinay is also the author of *The Keshav Way* and *Keshav*.

Connect with Vinay on Social Media:

@the.keshav.way

Vinay's Website:

www.vinaysutaria.com

CPSIA information can be obtained
at www.ICGtesting.com
Printed in the USA
LVHW031124141122
732907LV00005B/104

9 781838 198541